Beginning Reactive Programming with Swift

Using RxSwift, Amazon Web Services, and JSON with iOS and macOS

Jesse Feiler

Apress®

Beginning Reactive Programming with Swift: Using RxSwift, Amazon Web Services, and JSON with iOS and macOS

Jesse Feiler
Plattsburgh, New York, USA

ISBN-13 (pbk): 978-1-4842-3620-8   ISBN-13 (electronic): 978-1-4842-3621-5
https://doi.org/10.1007/978-1-4842-3621-5

Library of Congress Control Number: 2018955902

Managing Director, Apress Media LLC: Welmoed Spahr
Acquisitions Editor: Aaron Black
Development Editor: James Markham
Coordinating Editor: Jessica Vakili

Cover designed by eStudioCalamar

Cover image designed by Freepik (www.freepik.com)

Distributed to the book trade worldwide by Springer Science+Business Media New York, 233 Spring Street, 6th Floor, New York, NY 10013. Phone 1-800-SPRINGER, fax (201) 348-4505, email orders-ny@springer-sbm.com, or visit www.springeronline.com. Apress Media, LLC is a California LLC and the sole member (owner) is Springer Science + Business Media Finance Inc (SSBM Finance Inc). SSBM Finance Inc is a **Delaware** corporation.

For information on translations, please email rights@apress.com, or visit http://www.apress.com/rights-permissions.

Apress titles may be purchased in bulk for academic, corporate, or promotional use. eBook versions and licenses are also available for most titles. For more information, reference our Print and eBook Bulk Sales web page at http://www.apress.com/bulk-sales.

Any source code or other supplementary material referenced by the author in this book is available to readers on GitHub via the book's product page, located at www.apress.com/978-1-4842-3620-8. For more detailed information, please visit http://www.apress.com/source-code.

Printed on acid-free paper

Table of Contents

About the Author

Jesse Feiler is a developer, consultant, trainer, and author specializing in database technologies and location-based apps. He is the creator of Minutes Machine, the meeting-management app, as well as the Saranac River Trail app, a guide to the trail that includes location-based updates as well as social media tools. His apps are available in the App Store and are published by Champlain Arts Corp. Jesse is heard regularly on WAMC Public Radio for the Northeast's *The Roundtable.* He is founder of Friends of Saranac River Trail, Inc. A native of Washington, D.C., he has lived in New York City and currently lives in Plattsburgh, NY.

About the Technical Reviewer

A passionate developer and experience enthusiast, **Aaron Crabtree** has been involved in mobile development since the dawn of the mobile device. He has written and provided technical editing for a variety of books on the topic, as well as taken the lead on some very cool cutting-edge projects over the years. His latest endeavor, building apps for augmented reality devices, has flung him back where he wants to be: an early adopter in an environment that changes day-by-day as new innovation hits the market. Hit him up on Twitter, where he tweets about all things mobile and AR: @aaron_crabtree.

Introduction

As technologies change, we see how basic patterns recur over time. In many ways, there aren't that many new things to learn — just new variations and combinations of existing technologies and concepts. (See my book "Learn Computer Science with Swift" for more on the patterns that recur).

As always, there are many people to thank for helping on this book. Most important are the people who have contributed to the technologies. When it comes to the many open source technologies (including ReactiveX and its projects), there are more and more people working on the technologies, and that makes it easier for everyone.

Closer to home, Aaron Crabtree has provided very helpful and watchful comments on the manuscript. And, as always, Carole Jelen at Waterside Productions has helped make this book possible.

PART I

Building Composite Apps with Swift

CHAPTER 1

Building Blocks: Projects, Workspaces, Extensions, Delegates, and Frameworks

Building apps today isn't really about writing code. You may have learned how to write code in school or at a bootcamp intensive workshop, and those experiences are valuable ways to learn about the principles of coding. However, when you start your first coding job, you may find that you're asked to correct a typo in the title of a report that an existing app produces. It's a simple job that you can divide into two parts.

First, find where the typo is (a basic app can easily have many thousands of lines of code—Windows is estimated to have 50 million lines). It might not take long to find a typo in a single line of code, but how long does it take to find the line of code in the first place?

Second, fix the typo.

A month later, after you have finished the task of changing the title typo, you may find yourself actually building an app. That job, too, can be divided into several component parts.

© Jesse Feiler 2018
J. Feiler, *Beginning Reactive Programming with Swift*,
https://doi.org/10.1007/978-1-4842-3621-5_1

First, implement a user authentication process. You can do this using
the Facebook API or using some open source code from a trusted web
source. You just have to find the code or API and then put it into your app.

Second, you need to implement your app's functionality that comes
into play after the authentication process is complete. Depending on what
the app is, you may have to write it from scratch, but chances are that you'll
find yourself revising existing code from a similar project.

Third, you may take your new app and port it to a different platform.

Coding today is often about reading and understanding existing code
and then reusing it in new apps and new combinations. Yes, there is a lot
of from-scratch coding going on, but there's also a lot of reuse of existing
code happening in the development world.

A number of factors have come together to create and support this
world of reusable and repurposed code, which, after all, represents many,
many hours of effort by many, many people. Reusing analysis and code is
just as important as reusing and recycling natural resources. In the case of
code, reuse means not reinventing the wheel. By not starting from scratch
each time an app is created, the entire world of software development can
move forward.

This chapter will provide an overview of how this world of reusable
code functions—particularly from the vantage point of iOS, tvOS, macOS,
and watchOS. You will find an overview of the reusable code building
blocks, along with an overview of how you can put them together using
Xcode and other tools that are part of the Apple developer's standard
toolkit. There are three parts to the chapter:

- **Component Architecture Overview** gives you an idea
  of what it's like to build apps from components.

- **Looking at the iOS and macOS Building Blocks**
  provides an overview of what those blocks are.

- **Building with the Building Blocks** provides an
  overview of how to put them together.

Component Architecture Overview

Since the beginning of the computer age in the 1940s, there has been a development backlog of projects waiting to be done. (A companion backlog accompanied the rise of the web.) The need for software seemed unstoppable. Various strategies emerged, and *components* were a key part of many of them, both for the web and for software in general.

The idea was that building complete websites, programs, and apps from scratch was an unsustainable model. There had to be some way of speeding things up by reusing code that had already been written and debugged. The problem with this simple idea was that it wasn't possible to easily reuse code—changes always needed to be made.

One way of reusing code to speed up the development process was to take existing code and extract its key functions and features. These elements could be reused more easily than an entire code base. This was the beginning of component software development.

As time passed, these reusable extracts began to be used in two different ways:

- **Use a framework or shell.** In this model, there is a framework into which you can plug components.

    The framework model was popular in the 1990s; IBM's Software Object Model (SOM) was one of the first. Microsoft entered the component software world with Object Linking and Embedding (OLE) and Component Object Model (COM). A consortium of Apple, IBM, and WordPerfect worked on OpenDoc. All of these were frameworks into which you could plug specialized components (from the user's point of view, most were documents into which you could plug components).

- **Build a product from components.** In this model, you combine a number of reusable components (off-the-shelf or written specifically for the project) to make a single product. There usually isn't a framework or container as a shell; in some projects, there is indeed such an overarching container or shell, but it may be created specially for each project.

Regardless of the component model you're working with, there is a critical issue that crops up as soon as you start thinking about components: What language will you use? In today's world, the languages for iOS (and macOS) are Swift and Objective-C. However, one of the features of component architecture is that in some cases you can mix different languages, as you will see in the "Command-Line Integration" section later in this chapter.

Looking at the iOS and macOS Building Blocks

The building blocks in this section are all built in the Swift and Objective-C languages for iOS and macOS, and with APIs such as UIKit for iOS and AppKit for macOS, as well as their companions. This section will provide a brief overview of the building blocks; for more information, look on developer.apple.com.

Extensions

Extensions in Swift let you add functionality to an existing class, structure, enumeration, or protocol type. You can find an example in the *Adopting Drag and Drop in a Custom View* sample code on developer.apple.com. The drag-and-drop functionality is defined in protocols (see the following section for more on protocols and delegates) and implemented in extensions.

In Figure 1-1, you can see an app that uses the code from the Adopting Drag and Drop in a Custom View sample. In this case, the basic class is a custom view controller (`PersonnelViewController`). There is an extension defined as follows:

```
extension PersonnelViewController: UIDragInteractionDelegate {
```

Each extension is in a file that references the base class (the class that is to be extended). As you can see in Figure 1-1, the names of those files are

```
PersonnelViewController+Drag
PersonnelViewController+Drop
```

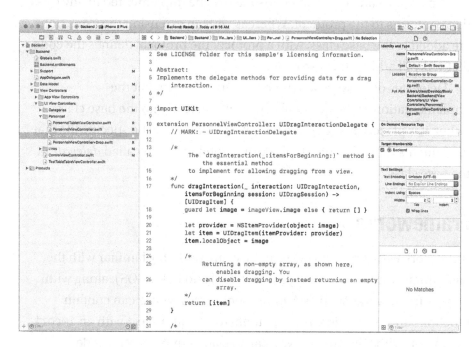

Figure 1-1. *Using extensions in a Swift class*

At runtime, you can reference the functions and other members of the extension just as you would reference elements of the class.

Extensions can be added to base classes and other structures for which you only have the API and not the source code.

Delegates and Protocols

Delegates and protocols work together. In the declaration of a class or other structure, you see the superclass (if any) in the declaration, as in the following declaration for a subclass of UIDocument in iOS:

```
class MyDocument: UIDocument {
```

A protocol can define functions that will be implemented in any class that conforms to the protocol. Whereas with an extension the extensions are added to the base class, with a protocol the protocol defines the code that *you* will add to the base class.

Delegates often work together with protocols so that the implementation of the protocol code is not placed into the base class; rather, it is placed in a separate file called a *delegate*. The specific file that implements the protocol is typically assigned to a field called *delegate* in the base class.

Frameworks

If you work with iOS or macOS a lot, you are probably familiar with the basic frameworks, such as AppKit (macOS) and UIKit (iOS), along with smaller frameworks such as AddressBook. Frameworks can contain functions and properties. You add them to a Swift project with an import statement; with Objective-C, you can use an #import or #include statement. (In Objective-C, the #import directive imports the framework once; #include may import it several times.)

Building with the Building Blocks

You can use delegates and protocols, extensions, and frameworks within an Xcode project. You can use a workspace to combine several projects, and you can use other tools to combine multiple components. Both workspaces and the combinations of building blocks will be described in this section.

Using a Workspace

With a workspace, Xcode takes care of managing the building of whichever target within the workspace you want to build. Targets may share elements from the workspace and will use them as needed to build various targets (such as for iOS and watchOS with the same workspace).

Building with Combinations of Building Blocks

The building blocks from Apple (frameworks, protocols, and delegates, as well as extensions) often provide a neat and elegant way to extend and expand your code. However, there are cases in which a single feature requires the use of multiple building blocks—for example, a feature might need one very big framework to be installed, along with a dozen or more smaller (but related) frameworks. Protocols and delegates are now commonplace in many structures, and extensions, likewise, may be added to the mix. Thus, implementing a new feature using shared code may require many additions to your code base.

Situations in which multiple building blocks need to be added to an app are common, and they can be difficult to manage. There are several tools available to help you manage such combinations. These tools use a structure that organizes the changes to your app so that a script or other tool can apply the changes in the right places and in the right order.

One of the most widely used of those tools is CocoaPods, which is the topic of Chapter 2.

GitHub has become the most widely used code-sharing tool and site today, and it is integrated with most package managers. Thus, the download of the latest GitHub version of the complex building blocks is done for you automatically as you run the package manager.

Package managers like CocoaPods use their own code and scripts to perform the integration. To do so, they—and you—must use some command-line code. If you are used to macOS and the Finder, you may not use the command line very often. Don't worry—the products hide most of that syntax from you. However, for the cases in which you do need to access a file or folder from the command line, the following section will provide some tips.

Command-Line Integration

Terminal, which is automatically installed as part of macOS, is the app that gives you access to the command line. When you launch it, you will see the basic screen shown in Figure 1-2.

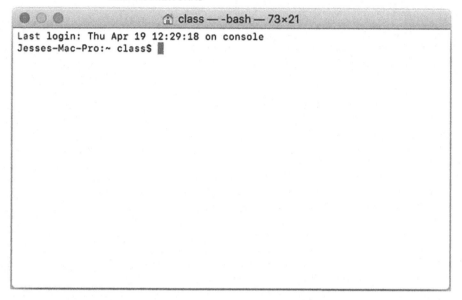

Figure 1-2. *Use Terminal to access the command line*

The first line shows you the date and time of the last login. On the second line, you can see the name of the computer you are using. You then see the identifier of the user you are running, and a symbol such as $ marks the end of the automatically generated text. You type your command after that.

Note   You can customize the formatting of lines in Terminal.

In Figure 1-3, you can see the first command entered into Terminal. It is the list command (the code is ls).

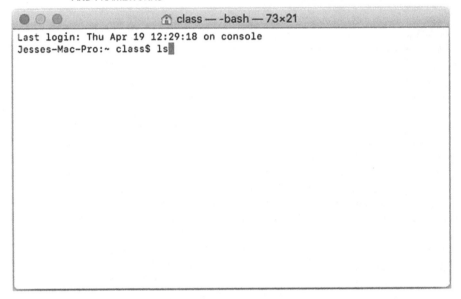

Figure 1-3. *Enter the ls command*

In a command-line interface, you deal with only one line at a time. You cannot copy or paste into previous lines of code, but you can backspace on the line you're editing. You end the line with a Return character, and the command is executed.

The results of the ls command are shown in the Terminal window, as you can see in Figure 1-4.

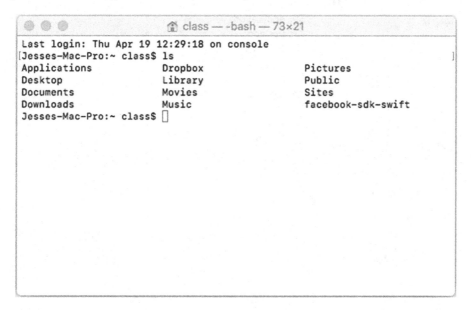

Figure 1-4. *Results of the ls command in Terminal*

If you look at the same directory in the Finder, you'll see the data as shown in Figure 1-5. The fact that the files may be in a different order doesn't matter. Note, too, that some files that are normally invisible in the Finder may show up in Terminal.

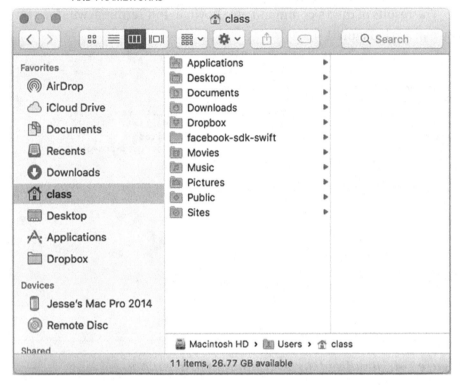

Figure 1-5. *Files in Finder*

There's one other command that you may need to use when you're
working with Terminal: You can change which directory you are in by
typing cd. You can then type in the name of the directory you want to
use, or you can drag and drop a directory from the Finder onto the line in
Terminal that you have started by typing cd. The text representation of that
directory will be placed into the line of Terminal code. As soon as you press
Return, the directory will be changed.

Summary

Xcode has a variety of tools that you can use (along with Objective-C and Swift) to build complex apps with reusable code, saving you development and debugging time. This chapter has provided a brief overview to get you started.

For more information, use your standard online resources as well as the discussion boards on `developer.apple.com`. For now, it's time to move on to the package managers.

CHAPTER 2

Using CocoaPods

CocoaPods is a tool for managing multiple components in an Xcode project. The basic overview is that you create your Xcode project as usual. You then run CocoaPods to place your Xcode project into a new workspace that it creates. Next to your project in your workspace are various CocoaPods with the updates you want to install.

CocoaPods can download the updates as needed from a GitHub repository, so you don't need to worry about doing that yourself. The CocoaPods tool keeps the versions of these public updates for you, but you can also create your own private repository if you don't need or want to share it.

You are responsible for managing a *podfile*, which identifies the updates to be installed. The podfile is the link between your original project and the updates that you install (and which CocoaPods can reinstall as needed).

This chapter will provide a quick overview of the CocoaPods process, with plenty of step-by-step illustrations. For more information, check out the CocoaPods site and documentation at `cocoapods.org`. For even more specific information, check out the Facebook and RxSwift chapters in this book; both Facebook and RxSwift are installed with CocoaPods.

© Jesse Feiler 2018

J. Feiler, *Beginning Reactive Programming with Swift*,
https://doi.org/10.1007/978-1-4842-3621-5_2

Install CocoaPods

This is a one-time task for you to do on your development computer. Launch Terminal to get to the command line. Install CocoaPods with this line:

```
sudo gem install cocoapods
```

You'll need to provide your system password. There are alternative ways of installing CocoaPods that you can find on the website, but this is the most straightforward for most people.

Finish setup on the command line by entering

```
pod setup
```

You will see some status information that ends with

```
Setup completed
```

You're ready to continue.

Create a Simple App (Single-View App)

There will be three parts to your CocoaPods project:

- You create an initial Xcode project as you usually do.

- You create a podfile to manage the updates and link them to your project.

- You update the podfile to install updates and new features in your project.

Figure 2-1 shows the creation of one of the simplest built-in projects in Xcode: a single-view app.

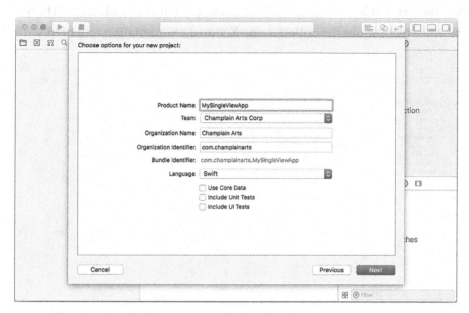

Figure 2-1.   *Create a new project*

When it comes time to generate the project files, you will need to identify the folder for them. You can create a new folder, as you see in Figure 2-2.

Figure 2-2.   *Place it in a folder*

When any new project is created from a template, test that it builds properly in Xcode with a device or a simulator, as you see in Figure 2-3. You can use Product ➤ Build or the arrow at the top left of the window. (There are other techniques described in the Xcode documentation and help.)

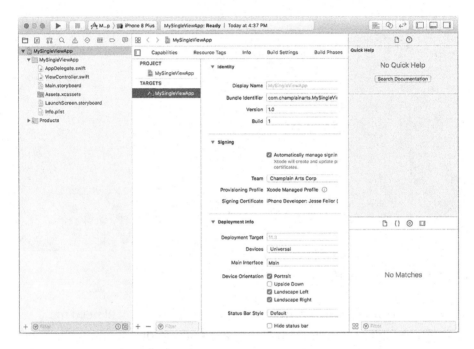

Figure 2-3. *Review the project*

Check the result on a device or simulator, as you see in Figure 2-4.

Figure 2-4. *Run the app*

Using the command line in Terminal, change the directory to the folder you identified or created in Figure 2-2. (Remember you can type cd and a trailing space and then drag the folder into the Terminal window instead of typing the full path name.) Figure 2-5 shows a cd command that is generated in that way.

Figure 2-5. *Change the command line to the project directory*

Using the list (ls) command, check that the folder you have changed to does in fact contain the xcodeproj file and the folder of source code created in the Xcode template, as you see in Figure 2-6.

Figure 2-6. *Check the directory*

Enter the pod init command on the command line in the directory you see in Figure 2-6. This will add a podfile to your directory, as you can see in Figure 2-7.

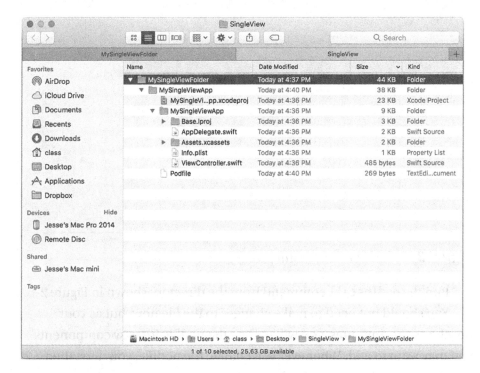

Figure 2-7.   *Add the podfile*

You can now look at the podfile, as shown in Figure 2-8. If you double-click it in the Finder, TextEdit will open automatically. You can also use a tool such as BBEdit.

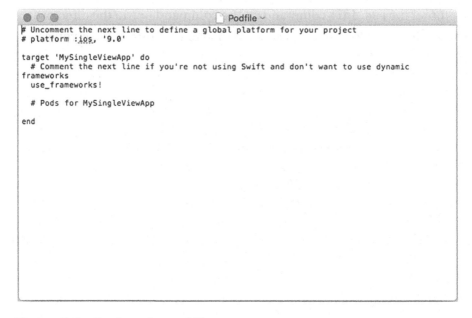

```
● ○ ○                          🗋 Podfile ⌄
# Uncomment the next line to define a global platform for your project
# platform :ios, '9.0'

target 'MySingleViewApp' do
  # Comment the next line if you're not using Swift and don't want to use dynamic
frameworks
  use_frameworks!

  # Pods for MySingleViewApp

end
```

Figure 2-8. *Review the podfile*

Run the podInstall command from the directory shown in Figure 2-5.

You should not need to make changes to the file now, but as your development continues, you will update the podfile for new components you may want to add. Whenever you change the podfile, you must then run the pod install command.

As you can see in the messages in Figure 2-9, there are no dependencies to install yet. But what is important is that from now on you should open the workspace that has just been created rather than the project itself. Close Xcode and look at the folder for your project. The file structure now shows a workspace and a new project for pods, as you can see in Figure 2-10.

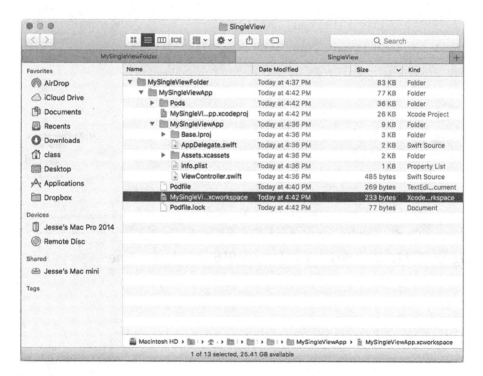

Figure 2-9. *Install and init*

Figure 2-10. *Your workspace window with pods is created*

If you are used to seeing files in the column view, you can change that in the Finder, in which case you should see files such as those shown in Figure 2-11.

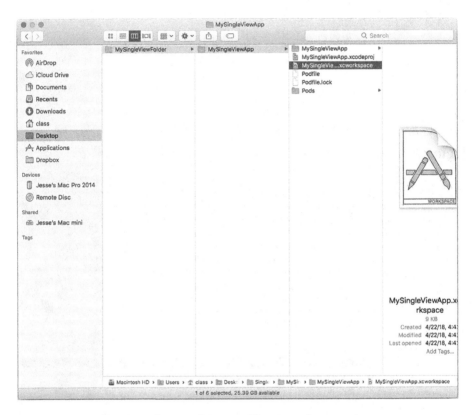

Figure 2-11. *Review the workspace files in column view*

Build your project again, and you'll see the pod code and your original code combined, as you can see in Figure 2-12.

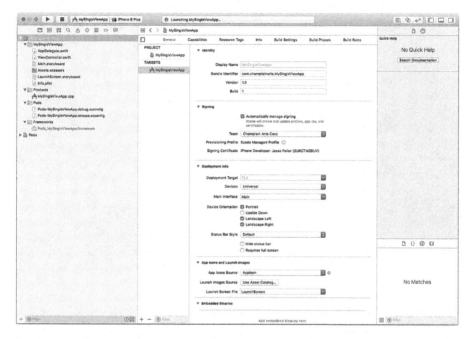

Figure 2-12. *Build the project with the podfiles added*

Summary

CocoaPods is a tool that is used for distributing many components and sets of components that are stored publicly on GitHub. This chapter has provided an overview of using this tool. Now, it is time to move on to another component that you will use frequently: JSON formats for files.

PART II

Using Codable Data with Swift and iOS

CHAPTER 3

Reading and Writing JSON Data

The building blocks discussed in this book almost all provide ways of sharing *functionality* across apps and often across platforms, as is the case with Facebook, Amazon Web Services, and reactive programming. This part of the book is different because it focuses on components and building blocks that let you share *data* across apps and often across platforms.

This chapter will focus on the specifics of JSON, which is one of the most widely used techniques for sharing data across apps and platforms.

Identifying Data That Needs to Be Shared

Apps contain data as well as functionality. You may think that a specific app has no data inside it (perhaps a game that users play by entering moves or data), but even that simple case is wrong. Every app contains metadata—its name, category, and description on the App Store as well as a record of related sales data from the App Store. Although that data is managed by the App Store and you as developer, it is still part of the app's overall data. In addition, there is app-related data that you typically place on your website.

© Jesse Feiler 2018
J. Feiler, *Beginning Reactive Programming with Swift*,
https://doi.org/10.1007/978-1-4842-3621-5_3

The data that we usually think of as being part of an app is the data that is built into the app itself: the code, storyboards, and app-based documentation and instructions. There is also data that may be stored, such as logs of moves in a game, high and low scores, and other data that is accumulated as the user uses the app. This is the data we normally consider when thinking about sharing data.

There are two types of data sharing for you to think about:

- **Sharing across apps.** You may need to share data across apps. A simple example is a photo that you capture using the built-in Camera app on an iPhone. You may then share that with the Photos or Files apps so that you can organize your apps into albums and share them with others. You may export the photo from Photos in another format (perhaps GIF rather than JPEG) to use it in a document or website. And so the shared photo may wend its way through several of your apps (as well as others' apps, if you send the document to your friends).

- **Sharing across time.** When you are playing a game, writing an essay, or creating a movie, you often want to take a break and save it so you can continue working on it another time. That requires you to be able to share the data across time. Remember that when an app is running, its data is stored in memory rather than in persistent storage (like a disk). Memory is a scarce resource, so it needs to be reused when you decide to do something other than work on your game, essay, or movie. The data needs to be copied to some kind of persistent storage so that it can be reloaded when you pick up your game or project later on.

Just to keep you on your toes, a lot of data sharing is of both types: across apps and across time. And as a further consideration, remember that when you share data across apps, you may also be sharing it across devices (from your Camera on your iPhone to Keynote on your Mac and on to your colleague's Photoshop on a PC).

Considering Security for Sharing Data

As people become more and more aware of the security aspects of data, it is important to consider the security side of sharing it. This is a common trade-off between ease of use for users and protection against allowing bad actors to exploit that ease of use for nefarious purposes.

One point that has become obvious is that trusting to luck is just not a reasonable strategy. Further, assuming that no one would be interested in your data is just as risky. Remember that people tend to reuse identifiers such as passwords so that even if you are sharing what you think is totally innocuous data, you may be sharing a user's banking PIN or password inadvertently.

Also be aware of the European Union General Data Protection Regulation (GDPR), which took effect on May 25, 2018. It governs data protection and privacy within the EU, but if your app is (or may in the future be) covered by the regulation, you must abide by the regulation.

The Challenges of Sharing Data

The data that your app uses when it is running is stored in memory in whatever format your operating system uses. From the developer's point of view, the data consists of variables, which are identified as types such as integers or real numbers, as well as the types and classes that you create in your app. When the data is moved to persistent storage (a disk, for example), the data is reformatted. All of this can happen multiple times for any given data within your app as it moves from memory to persistent storage.

From a practical point of view, data cannot maintain its formatting structure as it moves from memory to device and onward. That is why we wind up with various types of data formats depending on the medium and device. To make these reformatting processes work as data is moved back and forth, there are several challenges to be confronted. They are summarized in this section; in the following section, you'll see how these issues are addressed with JSON (JavaScript Object Notation, but it is used in many languages other than JavaScript) and other modern technologies.

Here are the challenges to be confronted in sharing data:

- Identifying data elements

- Managing inconsistent data types

- Exploring the document and structure issues

Identifying Data Elements

When you talk about sharing data, you have to make it clear what you're talking about. As noted in this chapter, "data" for an app can take many forms and can reside from time to time in many places, from a computer's memory to one or more persistent stores. Each has its own formatting rules, but before looking at that, you have to be specific about the data. What is actually shared is often a subset of the app's data—a log of moves in a game or the goal for a project in a workpaper.

The sharable data elements are often identifiable in the user interface using ordinary non-technical terms, such as *paragraph*, *page*, or *sentence* for words and *image* for graphics. If you can find a way to translate these UI elements into data that uses standard elements, such as characters of text or the binary string that represents an image, then you can share the data.

In general, the more basic the structure of a sharable format is, the easier it is to share, but there is a trade-off because the code you write to use sharable data that relies on basic structures may be more complex. Fortunately, over time processors become more and more powerful so there is often computing power available to do necessary pre- and post-processing of sharable data.

Managing Inconsistent Data Types

When you get beyond the basics of sharable data, you may encounter inconsistencies in data types. For instance, there is general agreement as to what an integer is (the mathematicians sorted this out centuries ago). However, what an integer is for a specific processor may be different from another processor's integer. This can let you specify a value of an integer that conceptually exists (for mathematicians) but cannot be stored on a specific operating system or a specific piece of hardware. This is one of the reasons why basic data types are used.

Exploring the Document and Structure Issues

If you look at the samples of JSON code, you'll see that they are very basic and that they only represent data. They do not provide any formatting, nor do they provide any logical structure of how a document might be presented. There are a number of document-based sharable formats, the most common of which is Extensible Markup Language (XML). It is more powerful when you are dealing with documents, but, as is always the case when the sharable data becomes more complex, it may be more difficult to share it across devices and platforms.

Looking at JSON

In today's world, JSON is a common way to share data. Its elements are simple and are represented using characters. JSON represents data as *objects*. A JSON object is delimited by brackets: { and }. Within an object, spaces and return characters don't matter except for the special case in which they appear within quotes.

Within the { and } delimiters of a JSON object, comma-separated name–value pairs define the elements of the JSON object. The name and value are both enclosed in quotes and are separated by a colon. When the value is a number, it is not quoted.

```
{
  "name": "Claude Debussy"
}
```

The value can be an array. In that case, the elements of the array are enclosed in square brackets and are separated by commas, as in the following:

```
{
  "name": "Claude Debussy",
  "works": ["La Mer", "Pélleas et Mélisande", "Images"]
}
```

Objects can be nested, as in the following:

```
{
  "French Composers":  [
    {
    "name": "Claude Debussy",
    "works": ["La Mer", "Pélleas et Mélisande", "Images"]
    },
```

```
    {
    "name": "Maurice Ravel",
    "works":["Boléro", "La Valse"]
    }
  ]
}
```

JSON is readable, particularly in small sections. Because of its
simplicity, it has no document-based structure or syntax checking. It is
easy to generate from data structures, which is the way much (perhaps all)
of the JSON code you will deal with is created. (Chapter 5 will show you
how to use the Swift `Codable` protocol to read and write JSON code.)

Because JSON is so commonly used, you can read it and write it
with many common tools. Some JSON code used for a navigation app is
shown in Figure 3-1 as it appears when opened in TextEdit. The spacing is
whatever has been typed in.

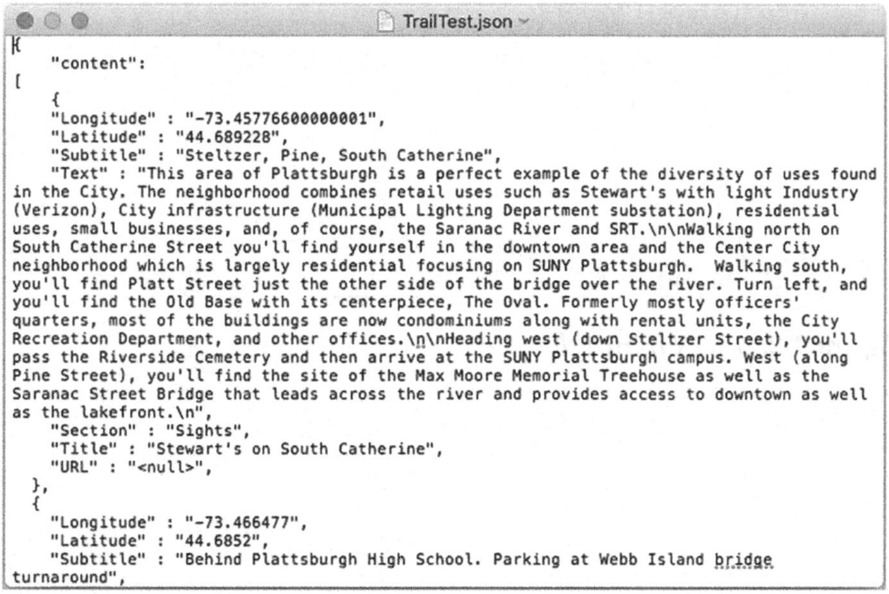

Figure 3-1. *JSON in TextEdit*

The same JSON file is showed in Figure 3-2 as opened in BBEdit. The text is automatically colored by BBEdit.

Figure 3-2. *JSON in BBEdit*

In Figure 3-3, you can see the same file opened in Excel. Note that the content is the same, but the spacing within the spreadsheet is done by Excel.

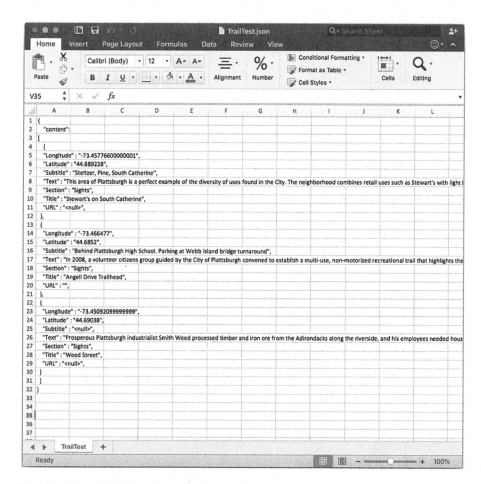

Figure 3-3. *JSON in Excel*

Finally, in Figure 3-4 you can see the same JSON file opened in Xcode, which applies its own spacing and coloring.

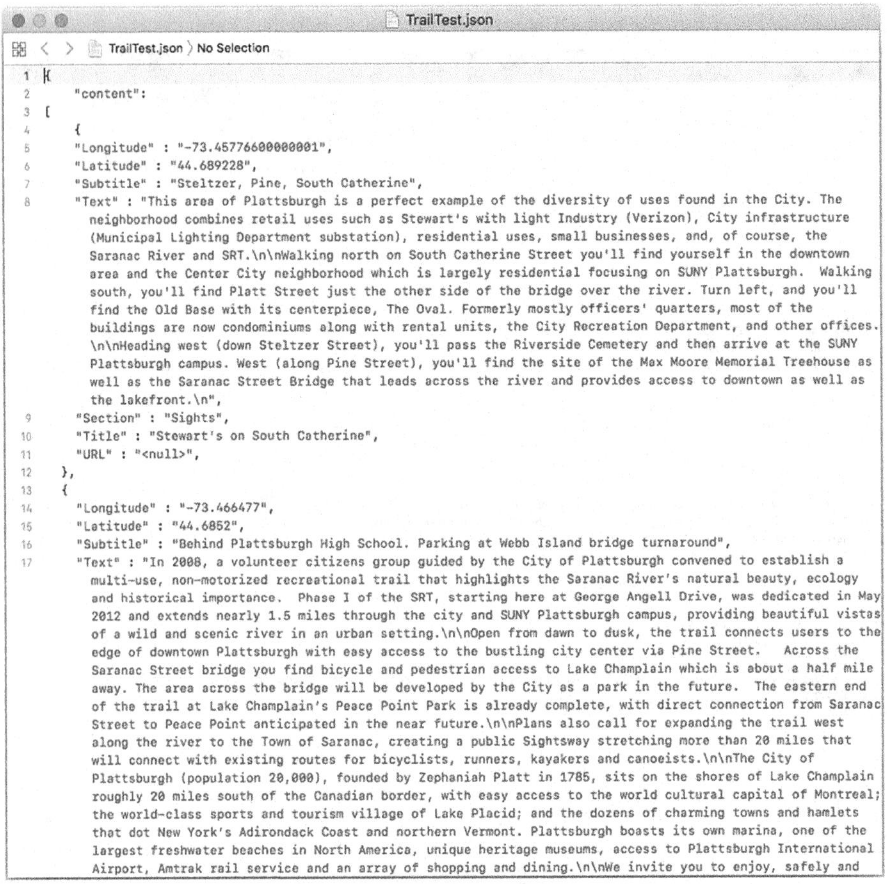

Figure 3-4. *JSON in Xcode*

Using JSON—The Basics

Despite the different appearance of the same JSON code in the different apps, the structure of the underlying code is the same, and it is easy to take the raw JSON code, which is based only on characters, and transfer it across any communications channel.

If you are creating the JSON code yourself, it's easy to misplace a quotation mark, comma, bracket, or parenthesis. Because JSON is so straightforward and is so widely available, you can find a multitude of JSON checkers and validators on the web—just use your favorite search engine.

The components of JSON should be familiar to you if you are already familiar with Cocoa or Swift. The comma-separated lists or key–value pairs are the heart of the dictionaries that are used so widely in the operating systems.

Built into Swift you will find code that easily converts dictionaries to JSON and vice versa. The next chapter will give you examples of that code. Furthermore, you'll see how to use the built-in encoders and decoders (in Swift 4 and later) that perform these operations for you without your needing to write any additional code.

Summary

Sharing data from one app to another, one device to another, or across time barriers is made possible by your using sharable code and standards such as JSON. The power of JSON is derived from its simplicity: it doesn't encode a document as a whole but rather lets you encode and decode basic structures such as objects (of any kind—not necessarily object-oriented objects), numbers, strings, and arrays. These processes are very fast and easy to use.

The next chapter will explore the built-in tools you use with JSON.

CHAPTER 4

Using JSON Data with Swift

In this chapter, you will see the basics of JSON syntax. You can use it with many modern languages, and Swift is no exception. In fact, Swift's integration with JSON is strong, powerful, and easy to use. If you add in Swift Playgrounds which is available on iPad and in Xcode on your Mac, you get a powerful cross-platform data exchange format that also is easy to test with a playground (so that you don't have to write an app—even a stripped-down app—to explore the data, syntax, and code).

In this chapter, you will see how to explore JSON with Swift Playgrounds as well as how to explore the iOS/Swift interfaces that are available.

Note These features are shown using Xcode 9 and Swift 4. These include significant changes from previous versions of Xcode and Swift.

Getting Started with a JSON Swift Playground

The Swift Playgrounds app is the perfect tool to use to get acclimated to JSON. In this chapter, you will see how to use a playground for experimentation. To begin with, you can create a playground and add

© Jesse Feiler 2018
J. Feiler, *Beginning Reactive Programming with Swift,*
https://doi.org/10.1007/978-1-4842-3621-5_4

JSON text, such as the examples shown in Chapter 3, to it. Using Swift Playgrounds, create a new playground, as you can see in Figure 4-1.

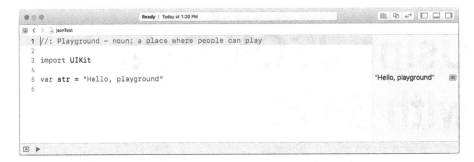

Figure 4-1. *Create a Swift playground*

Note   The examples in this chapter are shown using Playgrounds in Xcode on macOS. Xcode is the tool you use for writing code, and a project such as this one may be easier to work with on macOS than on iOS, but you can use either one.

Open the project navigator at the left side of the window by clicking on the icon at the top right or by using the View ➤ Navigators ➤ Show Project Navigator command from the menu bar. When you open the project navigator, you'll see the files inside your project, as you can see in Figure 4-2.

Figure 4-2. *Open the project navigator at the left side of the Xcode window*

Note   A Swift Playgrounds project consists of a single file in the Finder, but that file is a package containing the files you see in the project navigator. You can open the package using Control-click in the Finder or by using the right button while you click on the package. Working within Swift Playgrounds and the Xcode project navigator is simpler and more direct.

You can use the disclosure triangles to open the sections of the project. To add a file to contain your JSON code (or any other data you want to use in the playground), command-click on the Resources section and choose New File from the contextual menu. You can click the file name to change it if you want. Figure 4-3 shows a new file named test.json that has been created. There are two blank lines in it in the figure.

Figure 4-3. *Create a new file*

You can type in the file or copy and paste code into it (Figure 4-4). (The code in this chapter is downloadable as described in the Introduction.)

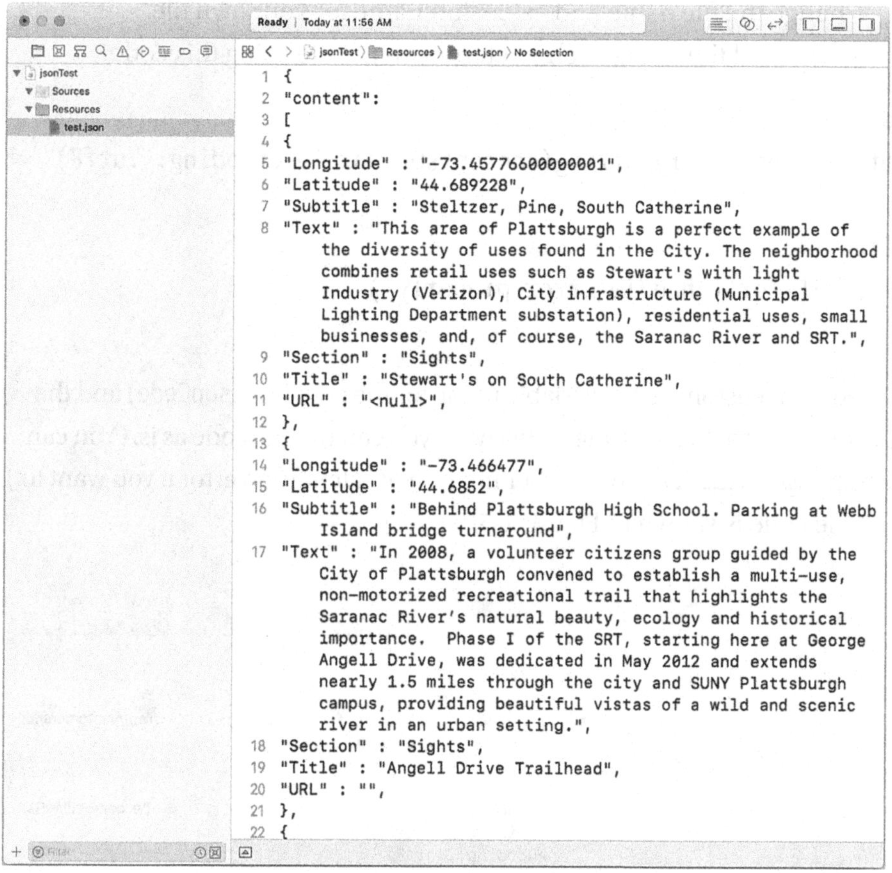

Figure 4-4. *Type or paste code into your file*

You now need to connect your playground to the file. Physically, the file is inside the playground package, as shown in Figure 4-3, but you need to read the data. There are two lines of code that you'll use (and reuse and reuse) to do this. First, specify the name of the file and where it is—inside the playground bundle. Here is the line of code:

```
let url = Bundle.main.url(forResource: "test", withExtension: "json")
```

Change the file name and extension name for your own file.

Then, read the string of characters from the file using this code:

```
do {
let jsonCode = try String(contentsOf: url!, encoding: .utf8)
}
catch {
  fatalError ("handle error properly")
}
```

You can customize the variable name for the content (jsonCode) and the text for the fatalError string. Otherwise, you can use the code as is. (You can also change fatalError to another method of catching an error if you want to.)

The code is shown in Figure 4-5.

Figure 4-5. *Enter the code to read the file*

When you have entered the code, you can run it, as you see in Figure 4-6.

Figure 4-6. *Run the code*

Check to make certain that you see the code properly and don't have an error. (This is the step that may catch you up until you're used to creating files inside a playground.)

If you want to show the content from the sidebar, a window appears, as shown in Figure 4-7.

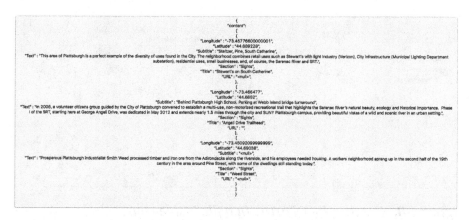

Figure 4-7. *Review the JSON code as it runs*

Using the JSON Integration Tools in Swift

What you have seen so far is how to create a file inside a playground and how to read its contents. The reading process is the same whether the file is in a playground or somewhere else—perhaps even being sent over a network.

What is more common is reading from a file and handling its contents not as a string but as JSON data. That is what this section will cover.

Integrating a Swift Array

Begin with some JSON code that you can create in an editor like BBEdit or in Xcode (or even in TextEdit).

You can start with a JSON array, such as the following:

```
[3, 69, 8, 66]
```

Note that the elements of the array are separated by commas and that the array is enclosed in square brackets. You can create a playground and then add a new file to it in the Resources section. Figure 4-8 shows how this will play out in this chapter.

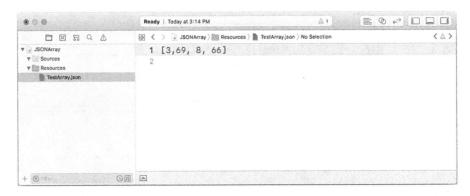

Figure 4-8. *Create a JSON array in a file inside your playground bundle*

You continue by specifying the URL for the file, as you have seen previously in this chapter.

```
let url = Bundle.main.url(forResource: "ArrayTest", with
Extension: "json"
```

Next, instead of extracting the data from the file as a string, use the JSONSerialization.json file built into FoundationKit to retrieve it as a JSON object. Note that this should always be done inside a do block that can catch a failure, as you can see in Figure 4-9.

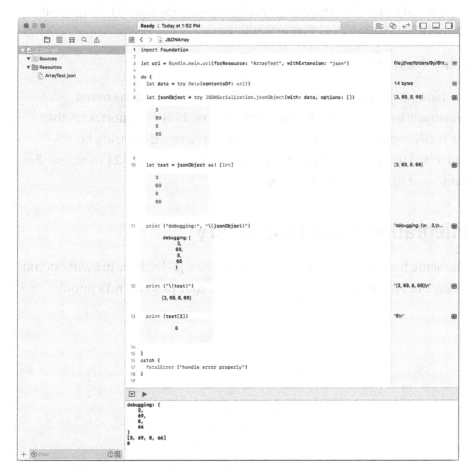

Figure 4-9. *Catch a failure*

Once it has been created as a JSON object, you can print it using Swift. What is most important in the code in Figure 4-9 is that after the JSON object has been created, it can be modified, as always, in Swift. For example, you can convert the array (in a JSON sense) to a Swift array of integers using

```
let test = jsonObject as! [Int]
```

You can see this in line 10 of Figure 4-9. (In practice, you would use as? to catch an error in the conversion.)

Several other lines of testing and debugging are shown in the figure, but perhaps the most important is line 13:

```
print (test[2])
```

Line 13 creates the test variable with the typed array, as noted previously in this section. The reason that line 13 is so important is that the JSON code that was probably specified as a typed-in string now is converted to a real object, and you can use the subscript [2] to access the data—just like any other Swift data.

Integrating a Swift Dictionary

The same basic steps apply if you want to use a JSON array in Swift. As you can see in Figure 4-10, you create the file in your playground's bundle.

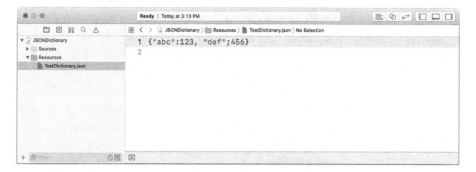

Figure 4-10. *Use a dictionary with Swift and JSON*

Note that the brackets are curly brackets, which is the style that JSON uses for its objects. Square brackets (as shown in Figure 4-8) are for a JSON array.

Note   This is the area you need to pay attention to. The rules of JSON and Swift are similar but not identical. For example, a Swift array has elements of a common type, but that is not necessarily the case in JSON. That is why you must always catch failures that may occur when using `JSONSerialization.json`.

Figure 4-11 shows the same type of testing and experimentation you saw being used for a JSON/Swift array in Figure 4-9.

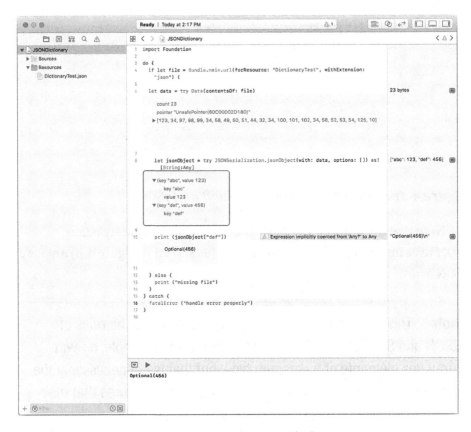

Figure 4-11. *Experiment with a JSON/Swift dictionary*

Summary

The ability to move data back and forth using a common syntax like JSON is important both within a single app and between multiple apps. This chapter has showed you the basics.

Note that beginning with Xcode 9, the Codable protocol is provided to further enhance Swift's JSON capabilities.

You have not yet seen the basic types of building blocks that let you share code and data across apps and platforms. In the next chapter, you will begin to look at very specific uses of these building blocks by examining Facebook logins that you can use in iOS (and other) apps.

PART III

Integrating Facebook Logins

CHAPTER 5

Setting Up a Facebook Account with iOS

In this and the following parts of this book, you will be dealing with the integration of an iOS project with a separate project, such as a project from Facebook, Amazon Web Services, or RxSwift. The biggest difference between this type of integration and the integration discussed in the previous chapters is that now the integration is more complex. It's no longer a matter of sharing data, messages, or data structures between apps; rather, you are getting parts of both components to work together. This chapter will explore the use of Facebook, which in some ways is the simplest form of app integration.

Note It might be useful to look at least briefly at the AWS, Facebook, and RxSwift integrations in the following chapters. Some of the techniques are used across other environments. Furthermore, being able to look at code in different environments that does the same thing can help you understand the major issues involved.

© Jesse Feiler 2018
J. Feiler, *Beginning Reactive Programming with Swift*,
https://doi.org/10.1007/978-1-4842-3621-5_5

Beginning to Explore the Facebook iOS SDK

The APIs discussed in this book change from time to time. In 2018, a number of them changed in response to the European Union's adoption of the General Data Protection Regulation (GDPR) and changes brought about by several highly visible breaches of privacy at many social media companies, including Yahoo! (3 billion user accounts compromised), eBay (145 million users affected), Equifax (143 million users at risk), and Target stores (110 million people with their credit card data stolen). Be very careful about relying on old technologies and code, but be particularly careful about relying on code that dates from mid-2018 and earlier. It may not reflect the changes that have been put in place in recent years.

As is the case with the other APIs mentioned in this book, a good place to start is at the developer subsite for Facebook—developers.facebook.com, as you can see in Figure 5-1. The API itself is always subject to change; furthermore, news and updates are shown on the welcome screen, as you can see in the figure. News and updates frequently change.

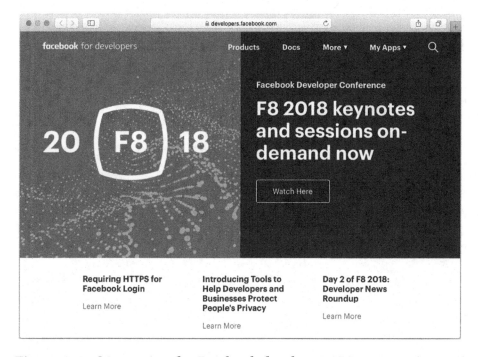

Figure 5-1. *Start to use the Facebook developer API*

Although the developer site for Facebook changes, its basic structure is fairly constant. Look at the black navigation bar at the top of Figure 5-2 to get an idea of how the site is organized.

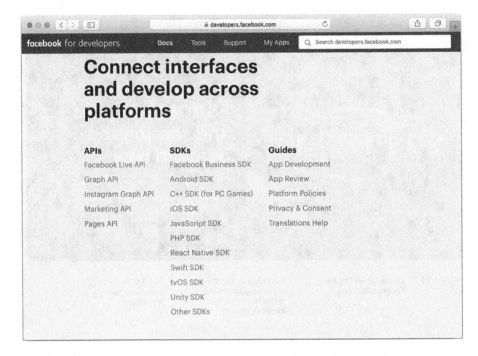

Figure 5-2. *Navigate through the Facebook developer site*

If you want to start working with Facebook iOS integration, look for the Facebook iOS SDK. You'll find it in the Docs menu of the navigation bar, as you can see in Figures 5-2 and 5-3.

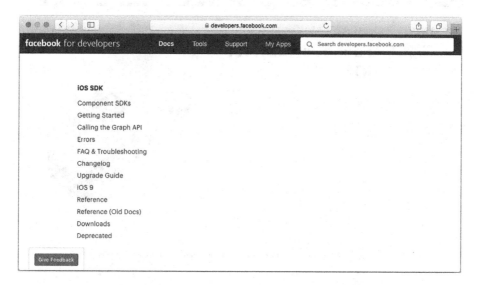

Figure 5-3. *Drill down to get to the Facebook SDK for iOS*

What you're looking for is shown in Figure 5-4.

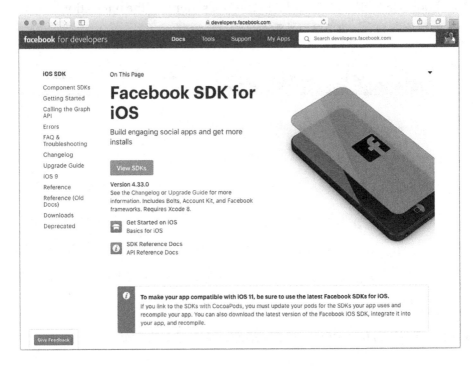

Figure 5-4.   *Explore the Facebook SDKs for iOS*

Looking at the Components of the Facebook iOS SDK

In Figure 5-4 you can view the major SDKs for Facebook/iOS. You can see them in Figure 5-5.

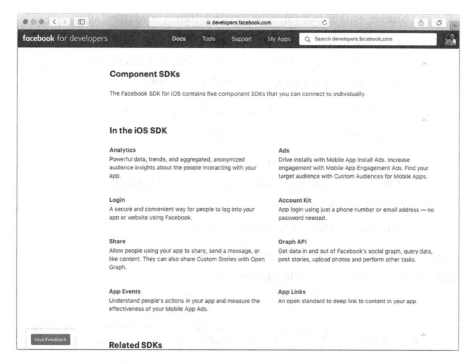

Figure 5-5. *Review the basic iOS SDK components*

As is the case with AWS, a lot of the iOS SDKs for Facebook are devoted to managing advertising and user interaction. The five primary SDKs are as follows:

- **Analytics.** You can see information about who is using your Facebook app. This information is anonymized so that you don't see individual information unless the user has specifically allowed that; however, you can see aggregated or anonymized data about your users. With Facebook, this is basically the information a Page owner can see in Insights.

- **Login.** These are the tools that people will use to log in to your Facebook app.

- **Share.** This SDK manages sharing, liking, and messages. (This is the SDK that many Facebook app developers start thinking about even though its implementation will require dealing with other SDKs as well.)

- **App Events.** This SDK lets you see the events and actions taken by users in your app.

- **Ads.** For many developers, this is the critical SDK. Share and App Events are what may be most important to the users, but Ads are often most important to the business manager.

As you drill down deeper into the iOS Facebook SDK, you can find related SDKs, as you can see in Figure 5-6.

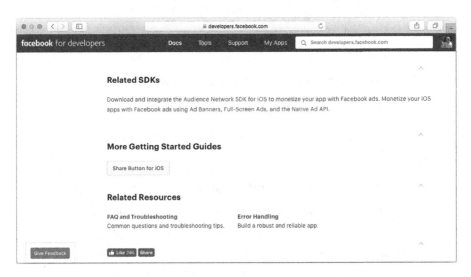

Figure 5-6. *See additional resources and get started*

The last stop on your overview may be the resources shown in Figure 5-6.

Summary

Integrating Facebook APIs with iOS requires persistent and complex tools so that Facebook itself, your Facebook app, and your iOS app function seamlessly together. In order to move forward, you'll use the steps outlined in the following chapter.

CHAPTER 6

Managing Facebook Logins

The first login procedure you need to worry about is the login for yourself as a Facebook developer for a specific app. This chapter will help you navigate that login protocol. Remember that there are many sequences of steps you can take to achieve your desired result—access to the Facebook iOS API.

Beginning the Facebook SDK Login Process

Start by logging in to your Facebook developer account. If you are proceeding from the previous chapter, you can now use the Quick Start for iOS button shown in Figure 6-1.

© Jesse Feiler 2018
J. Feiler, *Beginning Reactive Programming with Swift*,
https://doi.org/10.1007/978-1-4842-3621-5_6

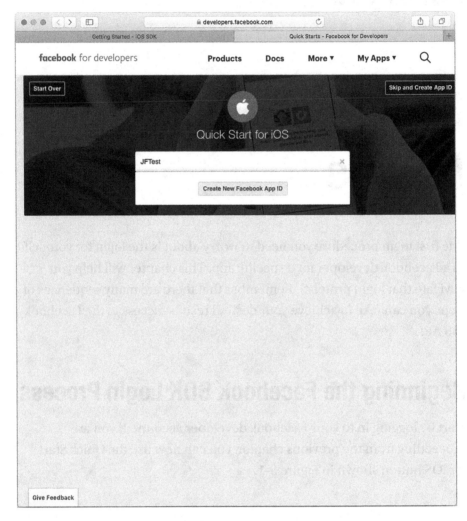

Figure 6-1. *Start by creating a new Facebook App ID*

You need to provide your app's name and your contact email address. (Remember that to get to this dialog you need to have logged in to your Facebook developer account, so that information is already part of the app that's being created.) Figure 6-2 shows the app creation step.

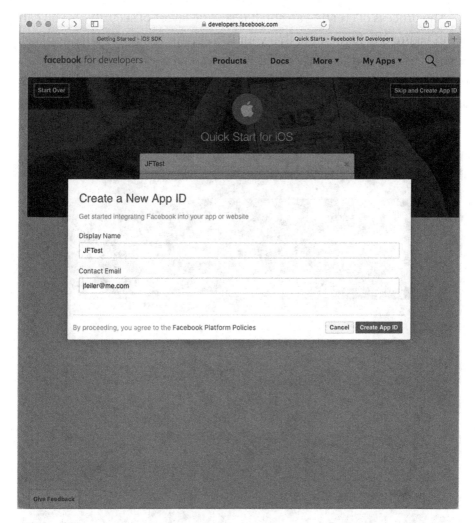

Figure 6-2. *Name your new Facebook app and provide a contact email address*

The process of creating an app has several layers of security, as you can see in Figure 6-3. Remember that your iOS app (or any non-native app) will have access to significant Facebook and personal resources, so security is tight and has been increased significantly since some issues arose in 2017 and early 2018.

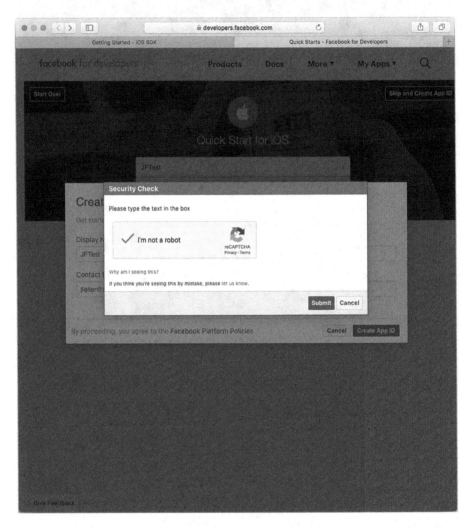

Figure 6-3. *Pass through the Facebook security process*

Providing Basic iOS/Facebook Integration

As you can see in Figure 6-4, you continue on with the Facebook for iOS SDK.

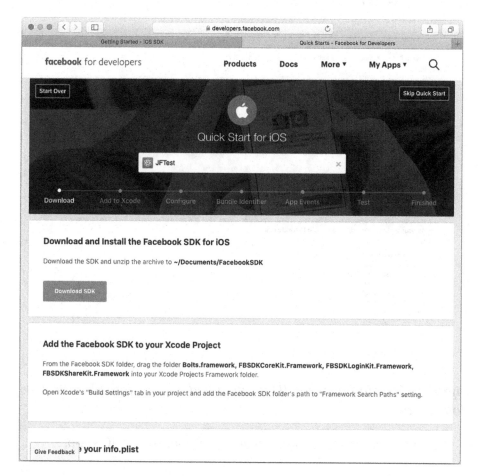

Figure 6-4. *Integrate the Facebook SDK for IOS*

The downloaded SDK that you have created, as shown in Figure 6-4, integrates your new Facebook app ID into the property list for your app. Note the code toward the end of section 2 of the info.plist, as shown in Figure 6-5.

Figure 6-5. *Your Facebook ID is integrated into the info.plist file you download*

The code shown in Listing 6-1 is standard code for any iOS app.

Listing 6-1. Facebook Integration with Your App's Property List

```
<key>CFBundleURLTypes</key>
<array>
  <dict>
    <key>CFBundleURLSchemes></key>
    <array>
      <string>12345</string>
    </array>
  </dict>
</array>
<key>FacebookAppID>
<string>12345</string>
<key>FacebookDisplayName</key>
<string>JFTest</string>
```

The Facebook ID is used internally; the app display name is visible to the user. Remember this if you need to change the name at some point: most likely you need to leave the FacebookAppID. However, if you are modifying an existing Facebook app to get started quickly, you will need to change both FacebookAppID and FacebookDisplayName.

Note   It is often easier to use the quickstart Download SDK button show previously in Figure 6-4 rather than tweaking an existing plist.

Connecting the iOS app to your Facebook App

The plist you download has the Facebook name inserted into it so that the iOS app can use it appropriately. You now need to manually provide the iOS app bundle identifier (which uniquely identifies every iOS app) to Facebook.

73

Beneath the code shown in Figure 6-5 and Listing 6-1, you'll see a form, shown in Figure 6-6, where you can enter your bundle identifier.

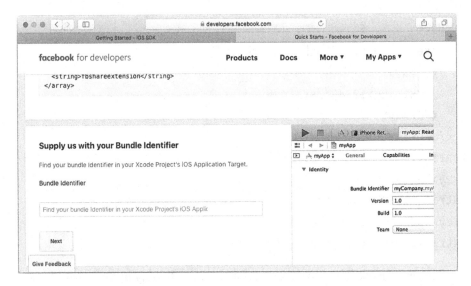

Figure 6-6. *Provide your bundle identifier from iOS to Facebook*

As a reminder, the bundle identifier is shown in your iOS app's general settings at the top (in the Identity section; see Figure 6-7).

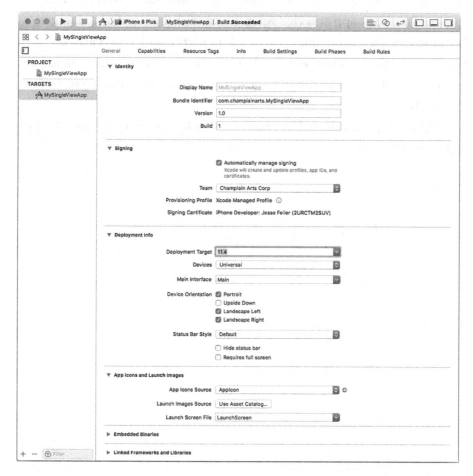

Figure 6-7.   *Use the iOS bundle identifier for your Facebook app*

Note   Always be careful about changing the bundle identifier. It is used in many places to keep the parts of your iOS app together.

Summary

This chapter has provided an overview of the connections from an iOS app to a Facebook app and vice versa. Be careful about making changes for their own sake. More than one developer has decided to "clean up" a bundle identifier at some point so that it adheres to an in-house standard or for some other reason. Chances are, that "clean-up" will cost you hours (or days) of work.

At this point, you should be ready to actually try running your iOS app together with Facebook.

CHAPTER 7

Adding a Facebook Login to an iOS App

With a Facebook developer account, you can add Facebook features (such as logins) to your iOS app. This chapter will walk you through that process. It is useful for many of the Facebook tools that you may want to integrate with an iOS app. Furthermore, the steps used to integrate Facebook tools are similar in some ways to the steps you would use to integrate other tools, such as Amazon Web Services (AWS), which is the topic of the next part of this book.

Also, it's important to note that there are a number of ways to handle this integration. CocoaPods (described in Chapter 2) are a very common way of handling integration. If you look into CocoaPods, you'll see that what you have is an automated tool for managing your Xcode project files along with having versions automatically downloaded from GitHub by CocoaPods.

The heart of the integration is Xcode, its files, and its frameworks. Although a CocoaPods interface is available for the Facebook interface, this chapter will show you what happens on the source code/Xcode side of things. Remember that regardless of the integration technique that you use, the same basic structure (updating and integrating your Xcode project) is what has to happen.

First, though, it's the Facebook login.

© Jesse Feiler 2018
J. Feiler, *Beginning Reactive Programming with Swift*,
https://doi.org/10.1007/978-1-4842-3621-5_7

Starting to Integrate the Facebook SDK with an iOS app

There are two components you need to get started:

- You need a Facebook developer account (see the previous chapter).

- You need Xcode and a basic familiarity with it.

Although you can work offline with Xcode as you develop an app, you cannot work offline to create apps for Facebook or iOS, because you need to interact with the Facebook and iOS environments. If you have anything other than an ordinary Internet connection (for example, if you are behind a firewall that limits the sites you can visit), check out the basic steps to get started to make certain that you don't need permission from another part of the organization.

Note Both the Facebook and iOS developer sites change from time to time, so you may have to search around to find sections that have moved.

Start by creating an Xcode project to use for testing. In this chapter, the Single View sample app that is part of Xcode will be used. Figure 7-1 shows how you can create it.

Figure 7-1. *Create a single-view app to test with Facebook*

Make a note of the app bundle identifier that is created based on the data you enter for the app. As you can see in Figure 7-2, the bundle identifier for this app is com.champlainarts.MySingleViewApp.

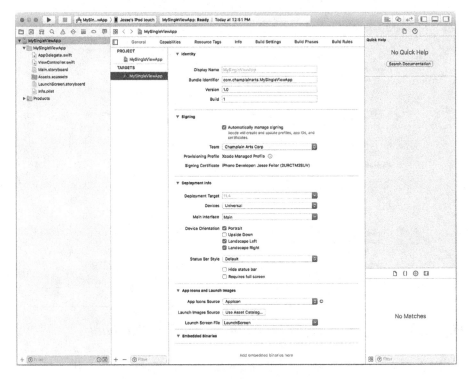

Figure 7-2. *Make a note of the bundle identifier*

As always when you create a new app from a template in Xcode,
run the app either on a device or on a simulator to make certain that it
works properly. Figure 7-3 shows what you should see if you run it on the
simulator for iPhone 8.

Figure 7-3. *Test the app*

Yes, a successful implementation of the single-view app shows nothing. As you will see later in this chapter, you can easily add a label. All you should be concerned with at this point is that the app doesn't fail or crash when you run it on Xcode.

Download the Facebook SDK for Swift

Log in to your developer account on developers.facebook.com. You'll see choices to download the Facebook SDK for iOS, Android, and PHP, as well as for other platforms. As of this writing, the basic iOS SDK is still written in Objective-C, but you can download the Swift version if you want (you'll see how to do that in this section).

The Swift version of the iOS SDK is under documentation. Once you've logged in, use the Docs menu item in the top navigation bar to get to the Documentation page, as shown in Figure 7-4.

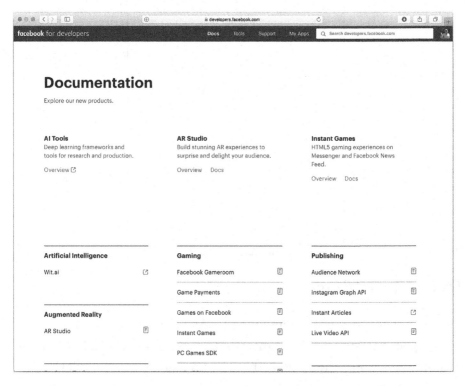

Figure 7-4. *Look in Documentation for the Facebook SDK for iOS/Swift*

You may have to scroll down, as you can see in Figure 7-5, to find the Swift SDK.

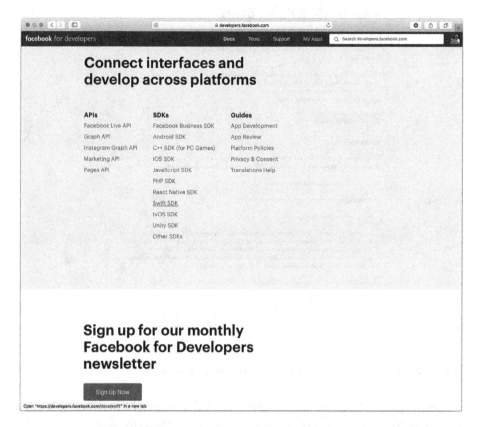

Figure 7-5. *The Facebook Swift SDK is available with all of the others*

Once you have located the "SDK for Swift" link, open it, as you can see in Figure 7-6.

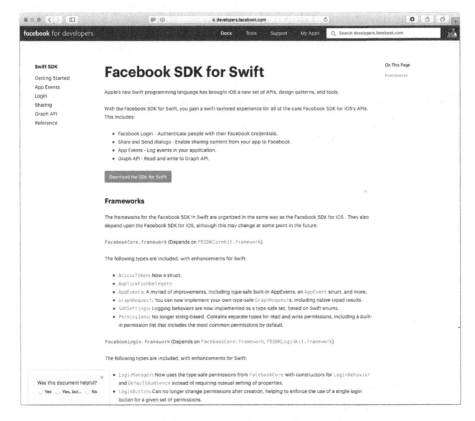

Figure 7-6. *Download the Facebook SDK for Swift*

The frameworks shown in Figure 7-6 are the heart of the Facebook SDK for Swift. All frameworks for iOS were originally written in Objective-C. Today, some of the new frameworks are written in Swift, but when you build a Swift-based app, it is not a problem that some (or all) of the frameworks are written in Swift. Thus, when you download the SDK for Swift, you'll wind up with frameworks that are often written in Objective-C, and that doesn't matter. When you download the SDK for Swift, as shown in Figure 7-6, some of the frameworks have enhancements specifically for Swift, so keep these files safe and just add them as needed to your app.

The download link in Figure 7-6 takes you to GitHub, as you can see in Figure 7-7. You can download the source code as `.zip` or `tar.gz`.

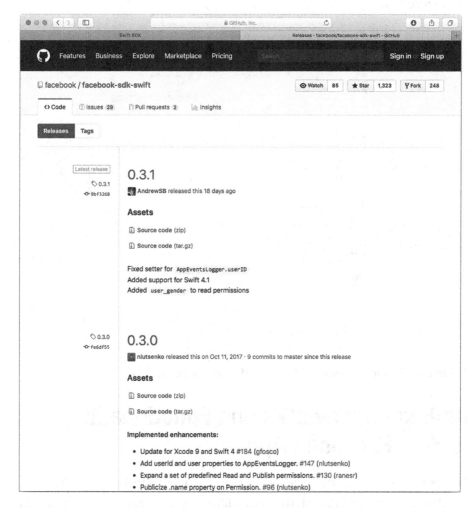

Figure 7-7. *Download the latest Facebook SDK for Swift*

The files downloaded from GitHub will vary over time both in content and in name. The downloaded files at the time of this book's writing look like Figure 7-8.

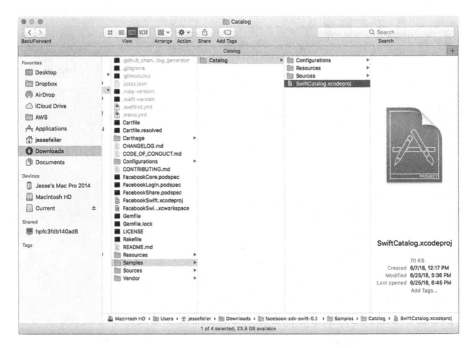

Figure 7-8. *Downloaded Facebook files from GitHub*

Adding Frameworks and Functionality to Your Facebook App

You can work around the issue of what file is where by using CocoaPods, but if you prefer to work with the actual files themselves, one technique that works for many people on many projects is to look for a sample file or app. In this case, there's a `Samples` folder containing a SwiftCatalog app. Many times (but not always!) the sample app will be updated for any given project before the documentation is updated. If that is the case, build the app. If you look at the project navigator, as you can see in Figure 7-9, you'll note intermediate files such as the frameworks are all built in the sample app.

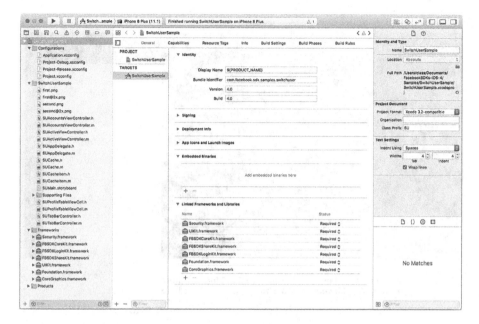

Figure 7-9. *Build a sample to get frameworks*

If you drag the needed frameworks into your own app, Xcode will put them in the right place in your project.

You can add new frameworks and functionality to your Facebook app either at the beginning or at any time as you work with the app. The My Apps menu in the navigator at the top of the screen (seen in Figure 7-10) lets you both add and reconfigure your app's components.

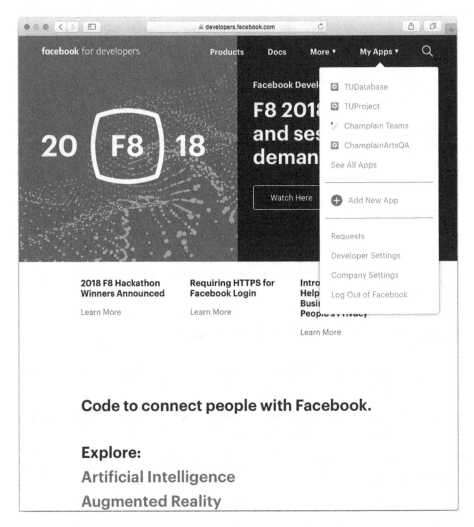

Figure 7-10. *Add and modify your Facebook app frameworks and features*

From your app dashboard (Figure 7-10) you can choose new products (features), as shown in Figure 7-11. This display shows you available products and links to specific documentation so you can decide what you want to work on.

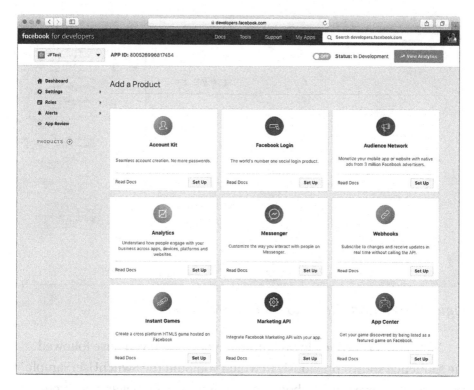

Figure 7-11. *Add products to your Facebook app*

Enhancing Your App

If you have followed along with this chapter, you have produced the app shown previously in Figure 7-3. It runs and displays its storyboard, which happens to be blank. In order to move forward, it makes sense to add something to your storyboard.

Go to `main.storyboard` in your app and add a label to it, as you can see in Figure 7-12.

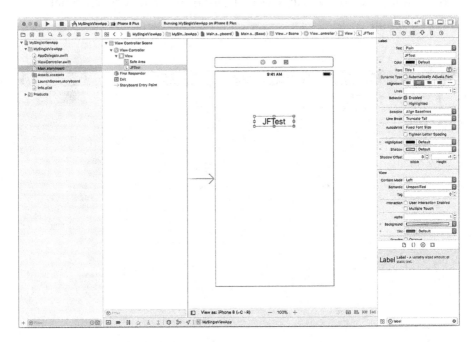

Figure 7-12. *Add a label to your app*

Next, add a Facebook login button to your app. If you have followed the sequence shown previously in which you built the SwitchUserSample example, you have the Facebook Login framework in that app and you can drag it into your new app. Alternatively, add Facebook Login from the products shown in Figure 7-11 by modifying one of your apps (shown in My Apps in Figure 7-10).

Once Facebook Login is added to your app, the code to add the button is simple. Add it to the `viewDidLoad` method of your app. (If it's built on the SingleViewController template as described in this chapter, the app has one view controller called `ViewController`.

The code is shown in Figure 7-13 and in Listing 7-1.

Figure 7-13. *Add the Facebook login button code to* `viewDidLoad`

Note   The basic `viewDidLoad` method with a stub is already part of the SingleViewApp template.

Listing 7-1. Add the Facebook Login Button

```
import UIKit
import FBSDKLoginKit

class ViewController: UIViewController {

  override func viewDidLoad() {
    super.viewDidLoad()
    // Do any additional setup after loading the view,
    // typically from a nib.
```

91

```
    let loginButton = FBSDKLoginButton()

    loginButton.center = view.center

    view.addSubview(loginButton)
  }

  override func didReceiveMemoryWarning() {
    super.didReceiveMemoryWarning()
    // Dispose of any resources that can be recreated.
  }
}
```

Rebuild your app (clean the build files first to make certain that you don't have some experiments lying around). Now, when you run it, you should see your label and the button, as shown in Figure 7-14.

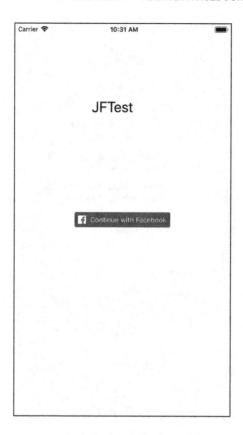

Figure 7-14. *Try your app with the label and login button*

Remember that you didn't just add the image of a button: you added the functionality of the login button, so when you run your app you'll be asked for permission, as you can see in Figure 7-15.

Figure 7-15. *Test Facebook login integration*

The login button should work now. Try it, as shown in Figure 7-16.

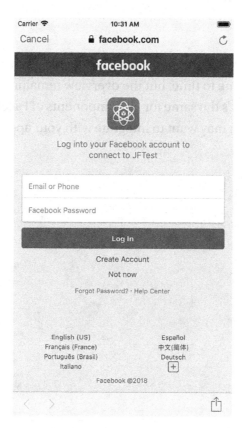

Figure 7-16. *Test the Facebook login button*

You can also test with your own Facebook account. In addition, you can search developers.facebook.com to get test accounts you can use so that you don't create fake accounts or interfere with your own account.

Note   Some developers test logging in with their own account but use the Facebook test accounts for adding information.

Summary

This has been an overview of integrating Facebook and iOS. The details may change from time to time, but the overview remains basically the same. And, in fact, it's the same for all components of Facebook and other frameworks that you may want to integrate with your app.

PART IV

Storing Data in Amazon Web Services

CHAPTER 8

Working with Amazon Web Services and Cocoa

In Parts III – V of this book you see how to put third-party components together with Cocoa and its frameworks. These components can be concepts, standards, or open source tools such as JSON, or they can be specific tools, such as the login using Facebook that is described in Part III.

In this part, a more general tool will be introduced: Amazon Web Services. (Coming up in Part V is RxSwift.) You will see an overview of how to create an AWS account for your app to use, install the appropriate downloads from AWS, and provide integration with your app. The focus of AWS integration is data management, but you can use AWS for other purposes as well.

Comparing Components

JSON is a tool for reading and writing structured text in a simple way. It is so common these days that many languages, frameworks, and environments (including Cocoa and Cocoa Touch) support the use of JSON for both reading and writing.

© Jesse Feiler 2018
J. Feiler, *Beginning Reactive Programming with Swift*,
https://doi.org/10.1007/978-1-4842-3621-5_8

The Facebook Login tool (described in Part III) differs from JSON in that it is designed for a single simple purpose: checking someone's credentials. Rather than the tight integration that JSON has with Cocoa and Cocoa Touch, Facebook Login has no integration from the Cocoa or Cocoa Touch side: You simply add some methods, classes, or frameworks from Facebook to your app, and then a Facebook-provided class goes off to check the credentials and pass back a yes or no for access. (This is a simplification of the process.)

Amazon Web Services (AWS) is a different type of tool with a different type of integration. It is not explicitly integrated with Cocoa and Cocoa Touch. AWS functionalities are critical to most apps, and they are provided in a number of different ways. They can be provided with code that you write for your app; code found in one of the many frameworks or libraries available on GitHub and elsewhere; or code and frameworks that are part of Cocoa and Cocoa Touch. AWS becomes the data manager for your app, and you interact with it constantly as your app runs (depending, of course, on the specific design of your app).

Note   For the remainder of this chapter, unless a distinction needs to be made, *Cocoa* is used to refer to both Cocoa and Cocoa Touch.

Using AWS with Cocoa

As noted, there are many ways in which you can integrate AWS with Cocoa and Cocoa Touch. In the simplest way, you use AWS (more specifically, one or more components of AWS) just as you would use the Facebook Login tool or even as you would use an open source tool, framework, or standard like JSON. In those cases, think about an iOS or macOS app that incorporates AWS.

At the other extreme, you can use AWS (more specifically, one, more, or many components) as the heart of your app.

In both of these scenarios, the user interface is envisioned as being built with Cocoa or Cocoa Touch. The question is, where does the implementation of the basic functionality of the app take place—is it in AWS or is it in Cocoa?

Note   It is possible to place some of your app's functionality on the Cocoa side of things and other parts of the functionality in AWS. Depending on your environment, it may be advisable to consolidate the functionality on one side or the other, but that is a personal observation and not a suggestion.

The overview found in this chapter may help you consider the possibilities for your app. Four points are worth considering:

- Sharing data with others

- Using data across platforms

- Playing to your strengths

- Playing to your users' expectations

Each of these points will be discussed in the following sections.

Sharing Data with Others

When you talk to people about apps, they commonly think and talk about entering data on their phone and letting other people (or themselves at other times) view and modify the data on another device—maybe even on a PC sitting on a desktop half a world away.

That common scenario that we all recognize is complicated to implement. Typically, the data is going to be stored somewhere, and that "somewhere" cannot be solely on the phone from which it originated, because it needs to be visible to people when the phone is out of range or even powered off.

One of the most common ways of storing this persistent data is in one of the cloud-based services, such as AWS, Box, Azure, Dropbox, or FileMaker (version 17 or greater). You can also use the web (particularly with HTML5) to store the data, but it must be somewhere that is reachable.

Using Data Across Platforms

There are many ways to store data that needs to be shared. People who have worked with data of all kinds and on all types of projects commonly agree that changing a data-management strategy is not easy, and it gets more complicated as more and more data becomes involved, as is the case with an old system. Too often, people skip over the "magic" that they expect to happen automatically to the data.

With the exception of a project that does not store any data—and never will—it's worth thinking about how data will be shared. Here are some of the basic considerations and suggestions for how you might approach the data-management issue. Planning for data-management strategies that will only be implemented in the future is far, far better than leaving it to chance (or "magic"). In other words, you don't have to do it at the start, but you have to have at least one plan for managing data in the future, even if that plan is to revisit the issue in the future. Just make certain it's a revisit and not a first visit to the idea of data management.

Note   This section focuses on data, but it is now possible to move some or more of an app's processing to the cloud. In fact, the distinction between data and processing is hard to define in many cases because one can frequently be converted to the other.

The basic data scenarios and possible solutions are as follows:

- None. No data is stored and never will be.

- One user/device. Data is stored only for one user and one device. This is generally a special case for temporary data. It would apply to a calculator app that remembers its last total (just as calculators do). You can use the Cocoa `UserDefaults.standard` to store relatively small amounts of data on the device.

   "Relatively small amounts" has grown over time, but Apple's documentation indicates that it depends on the device. This makes sense because devices get more and more storage over time. Reports of 4 GB being stored are found in web discussions.

   The data may be backed up with normal backups of the device (if they are turned on by the user).

- One user/multiple iOS devices. This scenario is easiest to implement with the user's Apple ID and iCloud. There is a limit to the amount of space available, which depends on what iCloud data plan the user subscribes to and how much other data is being stored.

   The iCloud data is backed up automatically as part of the iCloud service. Nevertheless, if one of the devices is not reachable, its data may not be uploaded to iCloud in a timely manner, and, unless the app properly handles iCloud conflicts (as with user resolution of conflicts), the data may not be what you and the user think it should be.

- Multiple users/multiple iOS devices. CloudKit is a good tool for handling this situation. Because it relies on iCloud, backups are done automatically.

- Multiple users/multiple devices (or one user with only a non-iOS device). This case is usually best served with an on-demand cloud service such as AWS, Box, Dropbox, Google Drive, OneDrive, or similar. Backups are part of the service.

    Not all apps need on-demand storage, but that is a feature available from most of the services mentioned here.

Playing to Your Strengths

With the availability of cloud-based computing as well as data, you can choose where to put each one. In the previous section, there were some suggestions with regard to data, but with any project it makes sense to make your choices not just on technical grounds, but also with consideration given to the skills and strengths of your developers, whether it is a team of 50 or just yourself.

Playing to Your Users' Expectations

When it comes to users' expectations of shared data, the word "overused" is not far from the mark for unrealistic expectations. But there's another expectation that is just as dangerous: an expectation that shared data will be structured and shared using the latest and greatest technology from the age of mainframe computers and sometimes even from the age of punched cards. Data structures have a very long life span. In part, that is the result of what is sometimes called "the drag of the installed base"—the need to keep things running even though times and capabilities have changed.

One benefit of using shared-data tools such as AWS is that you and your users may be confronted with technologies and interfaces that may be new to you all.

Exploring AWS

After considering the issues of shared computing and shared data, it is time for a high-level overview of AWS. This section will provide that overview. In the next chapter, "Managing AWS in Cocoa," you'll drill down a bit more into AWS and how to integrate it with your apps. Remember that AWS is a very rich set of tools and that there is much more to find out than can fit in these chapters. The goal here is to give you an idea of what is available so you can at least make the decision of whether or not to delve further into AWS for your project.

Note   AWS is a web-based technology, and that applies to its website as well as its technology. The screenshots you will see and the steps you will take in this chapter may differ; however, the general process will probably be the same. It's fair to assume that some of the AWS components illustrated in this chapter may be enhanced, new ones may be added, and some may be deprecated.

Getting Started with AWS

The place to start is `aws.amazon.com`, as you can see (subject to
modifications over time) in Figure 8-1.

Figure 8-1. *Begin to work with AWS*

As a developer, your interactions with AWS are done through the
console using the button at the top right. You'll find other links to the
console throughout the AWS site. You are able to browse the site without
logging in to the console, but to actually do anything, you will need an
account. You'll see how to set up your account in Chapter 10, "Managing
AWS Logins."

For now, explore the menu at the top left, as shown in Figure 8-2.

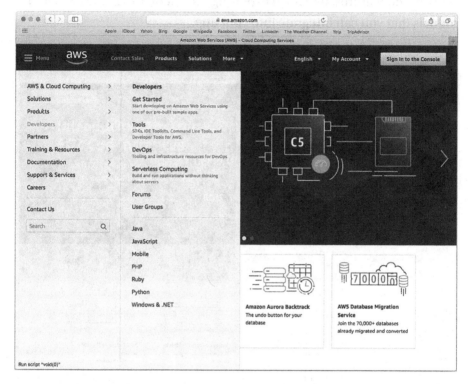

Figure 8-2. *Browse developer resources on AWS*

Figure 8-2 gives you a high-level overview of resources available for developers. The Developers menu remains pretty constant even as AWS changes.

The Products menu, shown in Figure 8-3, changes as AWS adds more products and features. It's worth exploring this menu to see the tools and products that you can integrate into your app.

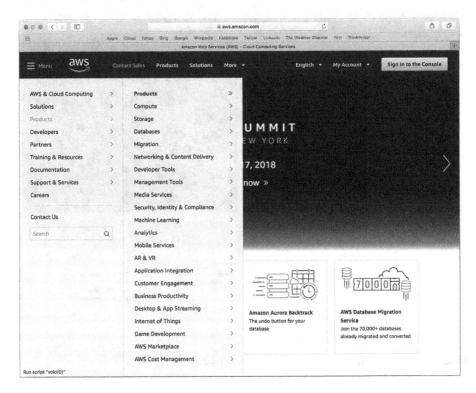

Figure 8-3. *AWS products*

Comparing Cocoa and AWS Products for Data Management

You can build a complete app from these AWS products (that's the idea of AWS of course). The only thing that's missing is the user interface. You can provide that with web-based tools like HTML5. However, for the most powerful and flexible interface, Cocoa and Cocoa Touch are the tools we prefer.

If you look at the list of products, you'll see that they are basic building blocks for the back end of apps. One of the most common forms of integration between AWS and Cocoa is data management, which is the topic explored in this part of the book. The tools available for data management in Cocoa are focused on individuals, so shared data management needs to be implemented (at least at this point) with tools found outside of Cocoa.

SQLite is built into Cocoa, but it is a personal data-management library; it doesn't manage sharing. iCloud is the Apple technology that handles data sharing, but that is primarily focused on sharing within one AppleID. (CloudKit does provide some broader data sharing.)

Core Data is a powerful data-persistence tool that is part of Cocoa. It is not a data manager; rather, it was designed as a front end to any data-management tool that conforms to the Core Data structure. Over the years, a variety of data-management tools have been integrated with Core Data in various forms of Apple products.

Summary

This chapter has introduced a high-level view of Amazon Web Services (AWS) and how its tools can work with Cocoa. AWS can be used to build an entire app, but commonly AWS provides a back end and Cocoa provides the front-end interface and functionality.

In the next chapter, you'll see how to log in and begin to integrate AWS with an app.

CHAPTER 9

Managing AWS Logins

In Chapter 8, you saw the wide variety of services that AWS offers (refer to Figure 8-3 for a list of products). When you use products that touch so many aspects of an app and parts of users' lives, security is critical. (This applies to your own apps, Apple's apps and frameworks, and third-party products such as AWS.)

Logging in to AWS is designed to be a secure process that compartmentalizes the different parts of AWS as well as the different parts of your apps. This is done with the login structure outlined in the first part of this chapter.

Later in the chapter, you'll find more details on how to integrate AWS into an app with Xcode. Because everyone works through AWS in their own way, you'll encounter many options and features that will matter to you and others that you can put aside for later (or never). You may want to refer back to the following items, found in the various menus, that may be important as you start to integrate AWS into an app:

- Login (Figure 9-2)

- Mobile Hub (Figure 9-9)

Looking at AWS Accounts and the Root User

You get to AWS at aws.amazon.com. You can browse some of the features and documentation as described in Chapter 8, but to do anything more (such as using AWS in an app), you need to log in.

© Jesse Feiler 2018
J. Feiler, *Beginning Reactive Programming with Swift*,
https://doi.org/10.1007/978-1-4842-3621-5_9

Note   The logins described in this chapter are developer logins that let you build your AWS assets. Once they are built and deployed with your app, users log in to your app on their own, or—in many cases—your app logs in without a user's intervention.

You can create a new AWS account from many locations on aws.amazon.com—just look for the "Create a new AWS account" link (wording, of course, may change over time). The portal shown in Figure 9-1 appears.

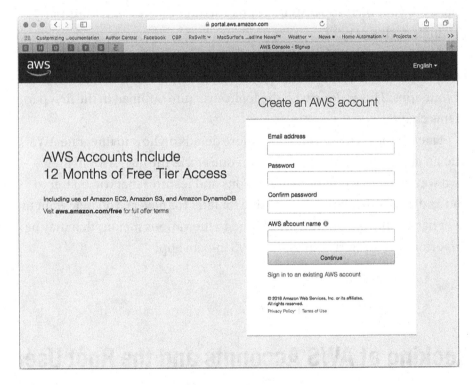

Figure 9-1.   *Create a new AWS account*

The process of creating a new account is pretty straightforward. As the little info button next to the "AWS account name" field will tell you, you can select an account name now and change it later. The identifier for your AWS account is not normally visible—your email address is linked to it, and that is changeable, as is the password.

Once you have an account, you can log in as shown in Figure 9-2.

Figure 9-2. *Log in as root user*

The root user is just that—the root user for the account. As you will see, you can have other users associated with your account. You do that by logging in as root and then setting up additional access accounts. This allows you to have multiple accounts within your overall account without jeopardizing security.

Note   As is always the case with a root user or superuser, do not use that login for anything other than true root or superuser actions, such as adding or deleting other users.

As you can see in Figure 9-3, you can access your account as soon as it is even partially set up. Use the "My Account" drop-down menu to do so.

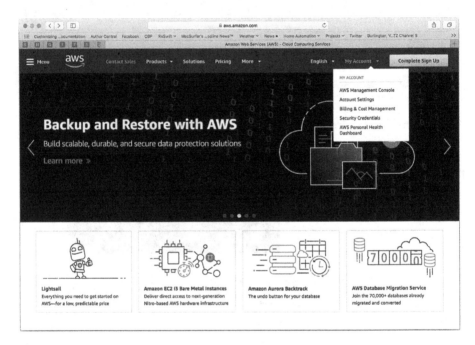

Figure 9-3.   *Access your account with the root login*

If you have not yet completed your signup, selecting any of the items in My Account will ask you to sign in using the portal shown in Figure 9-3.

If you select an item that relates to AWS Identity and Access Management (IAM), you will see the guidance in Figure 9-4 directing you to IAM.

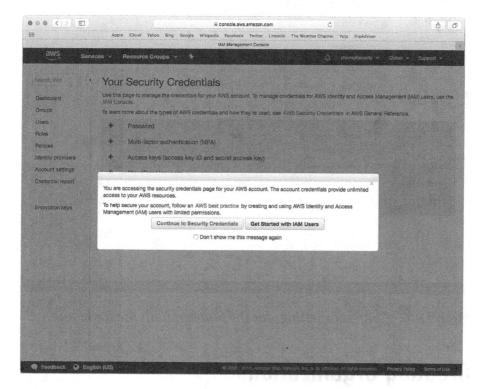

Figure 9-4.   *You are warned about using the AWS account*

If you continue to an area such as Security Credentials for the account (rather than settings for an IAM user), you are allowed to do so, as you can see in Figure 9-5.

115

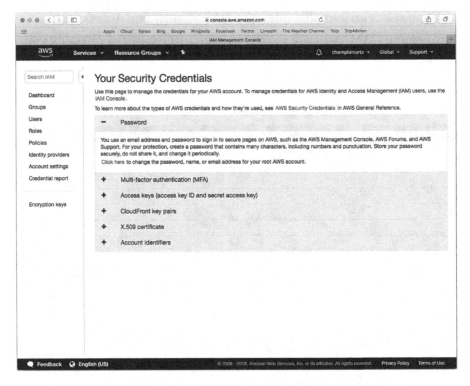

Figure 9-5. *Configure settings for the account with the root login*

Creating Organizations

You can create an AWS account, which has a root login (as do all AWS accounts). You can then add individuals to it. You can also create an organization, which consists of several AWS accounts. Do this from the account menu at the top right. It will have your account name. You have seen the account name (champlainarts) at the top right of Figure 9-5 and again in Figure 9-6.

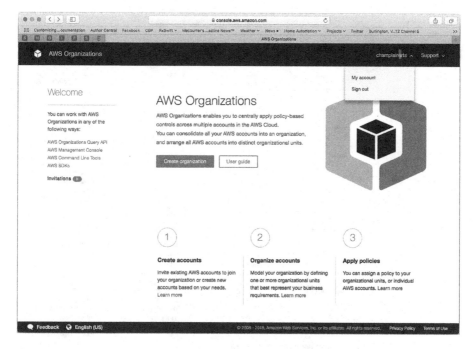

Figure 9-6. *Create an organization from your account menu*

Working with IAM

Because it is a best practice to not use the root user login, you may wonder how you use AWS. The answer is to use the built-in Identity and Access Management (IAM) tools. When you are fully logged in, you'll see a Services menu at the top left of the view, as shown in Figure 9-7.

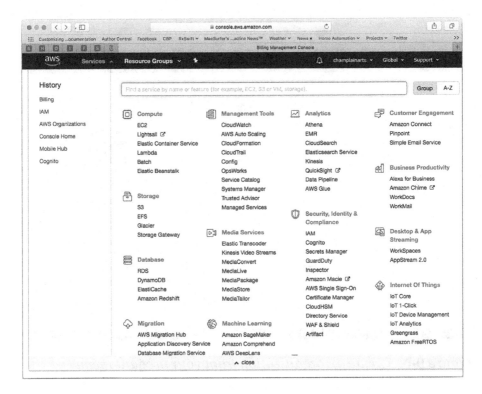

Figure 9-7. Browse Services

Note   Explore the various links in Services to find the options and your history. The items you will see include recently viewed items, so you will see different sequences of menus and their items. There is no single sequence of do-this/do-that that works beyond the single basic login routine. This chapter provides an overview, but experiment with the menus as you see fit.

If you select IAM, you'll be able to check its settings, as you can see in Figure 9-8.

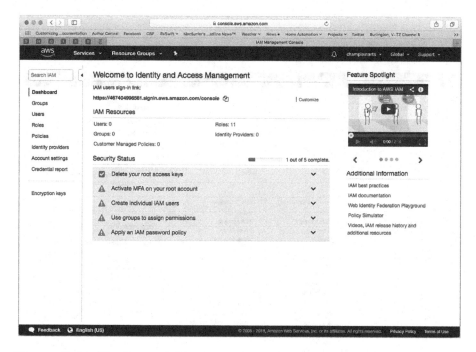

Figure 9-8. *Configure IAM*

To start working with code, choose the Mobile Hub service from Services (or History, if you've already checked it out, as you can see in Figure 9-9).

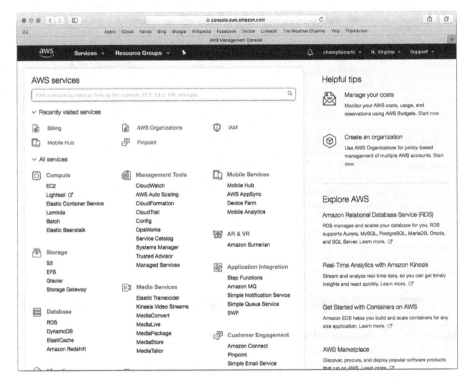

Figure 9-9. *Choose Mobile Hub*

Integrating AWS with Xcode

AWS Mobile Hub is where you work with your code. If you have a project, you can add AWS to it, as you can see in Figure 9-10.

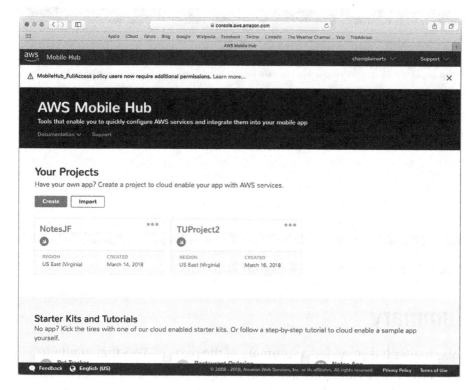

Figure 9-10. *AWS Mobile Hub*

Instead of creating your own Xcode project, you can start from an AWS Starter Kit, as shown in Figure 9-11.

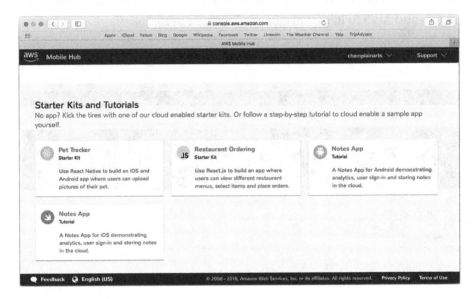

Figure 9-11. *AWS Starter Kits and Tutorials*

Summary

This chapter has provided a summary of the parts of AWS that matter to you as you start to integrate it into your app. It requires setup (such as in setting up an AWS account), and it requires that you have a project ready to have AWS added to it. You should now see how you can start to manage such a project in the Mobile Hub. The next chapter will show you how to set up a project for AWS. Once you have done that, you're ready to build out your app.

CHAPTER 10

Beginning an AWS Project

One of the most common (yet simplest) ways of using Amazon Web Services (AWS) is for data storage. If you have created an AWS account as described in the previous chapter, you can follow the guidelines and tutorials found in this chapter to build an iOS app that is integrated with AWS.

To start with, you'll see how to set up the iOS app and the iOS project that will be integrated with AWS. After that, you'll see the details of what to do. You can jump back and forth between the iOS app and the AWS project.

Setting Up the iOS App

Because this book builds on your knowledge of iOS and assumes that AWS is fairly new to you, the focus will be on the iOS project. You can build a project for iOS that uses AWS to easily get started; that will create a new iOS app for you.

That step is shown in Figure 10-1, so that's a good way to get started quickly. Once you have built your first iOS/AWS projects, you can easily start from the AWS side and then add the iOS component.

© Jesse Feiler 2018
J. Feiler, *Beginning Reactive Programming with Swift*,
https://doi.org/10.1007/978-1-4842-3621-5_10

Setting Up the iOS Project

Begin by signing in to the Console with the top right button on
aws.amazon.com or with the "AWS Management Console" choice from
the My Account drop-down (next to the Sign in to the Console button).
Both are shown in Figure 10-1.

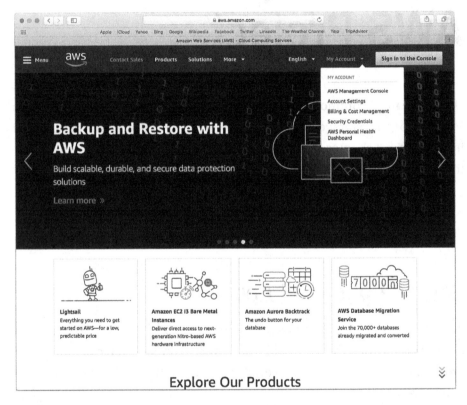

Figure 10-1. *Begin to manage your AWS account*

As always, you'll need to sign in to your AWS account, as you can see in Figure 10-2.

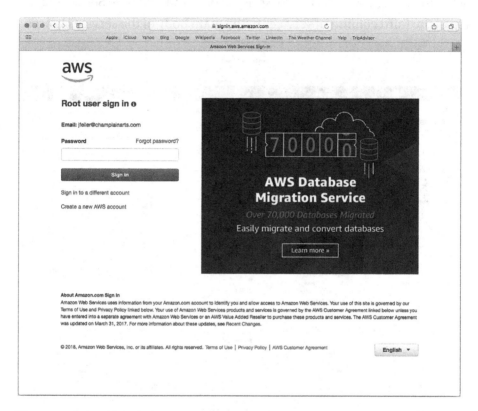

Figure 10-2. *Sign in to your AWS account*

Remember that although you can sign in to the account as the root user, you should use one of the other accounts you have created, as covered in Chapter 9. If you are given the option to sign in to the root account and you have specific accounts, sign in to a different account, as shown in Figure 10-2.

Once logged in, you can sign in to Mobile Hub, which is where you want to be. It may be readily available if it is a recent service, as you can see at the top of Figure 10-3. Otherwise, look for it under Mobile Services at the top of the third column of services in the main body of the service choices.

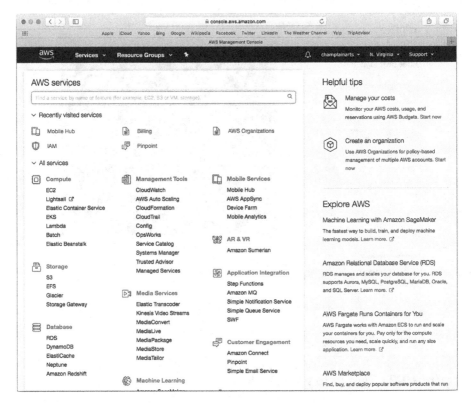

Figure 10-3. *Choose Mobile Hub from Mobile Services or Recently visited services*

Note   Remember that the available services will change from time to time as AWS evolves. You also can use the recents black bar at the top of the view, as shown in Figure 10-4.

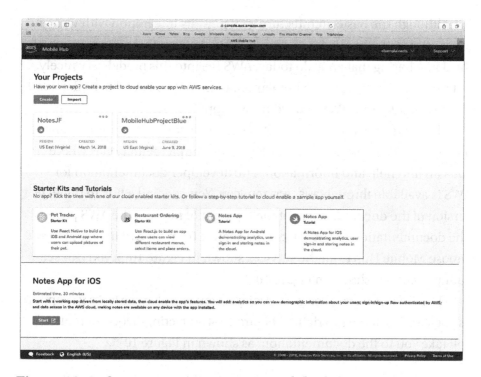

Figure 10-4. *See your projects in AWS Mobile Hub*

If you choose Mobile Hub, you'll see your projects listed (if you have created any), as shown in Figure 10-4. You can also work with a starter kit or tutorial.

Exploring the Documentation

The concept of cloud computing has been around for a long time. It was first referred to in the heyday of "thin client" computing, which emerged in 1993 and which some people considered to be an evolution of the "dumb" terminals that had been used in distributed mainframe computer systems since the 1950s.

Although the basic architecture isn't new, its integration with web and other modern technologies has provided a platform that powers much of the data-sharing that apps do today. AWS fits into this model very nicely, but there are specifics of the implementation that you need to understand in order to integrate AWS with your own apps.

The balance of this chapter helps you move forward to implement that integration. The first step to consider in your implementation is where you can find help and information. The developer documentation for AWS is available through `aws.amazon.com`. You can find a link to the PDF version of the documentation at the top right of many of the AWS pages. The documentation and its links may change from time to time, but if you choose Mobile Hub from the services shown in Figure 10-3, you can see your projects, as shown in Figure 10-4.

Note that when you see your projects, you will also see links to Support, as you can see at the top right of Figure 10-4. Selecting "Documentation" will take you to the documentation, as shown in Figure 10-5.

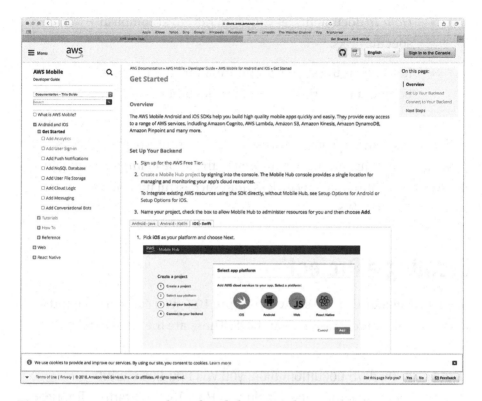

Figure 10-5. *You can download the PDF documentation*

At the top right is a button to let you download the documentation as a PDF file. As of this writing, the PDF document is over 400 pages long, so many developers choose to use the various online versions. The documentation is organized into four basic sections:

- *Get Started* (shown in Figure 10-5) is just that—the steps you need to take to get started. They are summarized in this section.

- *Tutorials* let you build apps or parts of apps to explore AWS. As you can see in Figure 10-5, they are available for iOS and Android.

- *How To* documents let you learn how to accomplish specific tasks.

- *Reference* is the source for information about what's behind the tutorials and how-to documents.

All of these may change over time. If you are just getting started with AWS, you may have the most success if you follow one of the tutorials. If you jump into the middle of a tutorial in the hope of implementing just one specific feature, you may be less than successful until you are more comfortable with AWS.

Creating a Project

From the Get Started page shown in Figure 10-5, you can start to build a simple app that integrates AWS and iOS. These are the steps to take.

Note   In the AWS documentation, you will find this startup information in several places, including How To, Get Started, Tutorials, and Reference. Until you are comfortable with the entire process as described in this chapter, you may want to try working with one of the sequences, as there are subtle differences in the sequences that can make it confusing to switch from one to the other.

To begin with, choose the iOS platform as shown in Figure 10-5. If you have not created a project (as shown in Figure 10-4), do so now and choose its platform.

Setting Up the Back End

The next step is to set up your back end, which manages the integration between iOS and AWS. If you clicked Add on the screen shown in Figure 10-5 you should be ready to set up your back end, as seen in Figure 10-6.

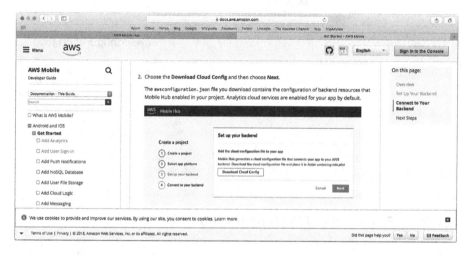

Figure 10-6. *Set up your back end*

Set up your back end by downloading Cloud Config as shown in Figure 10-6 to configure the cloud connection. Then, click Next.

Figure 10-7 shows a basic iOS Xcode app after the back end has been downloaded—either one you have created or a starter kit or tutorial. (The files should be in your Downloads folder.) The files in the project should be familiar to you. (By default, starter kits may be named something like aws-mobile-ios-notes-tutorial-master.)

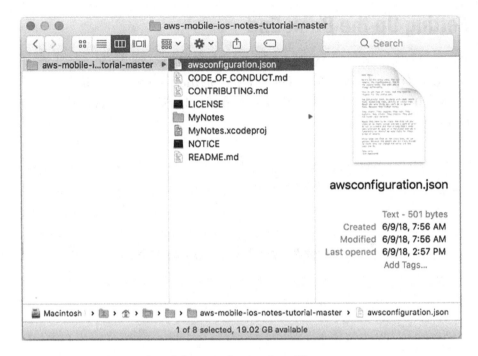

Figure 10-7. *Download the configuration file*

Look in your Downloads location for a downloaded file called
awsconfiguration.json. From the Xcode project navigator, choose your
app and then click Add File, as you can see in Figure 10-8, to add the
downloaded file.

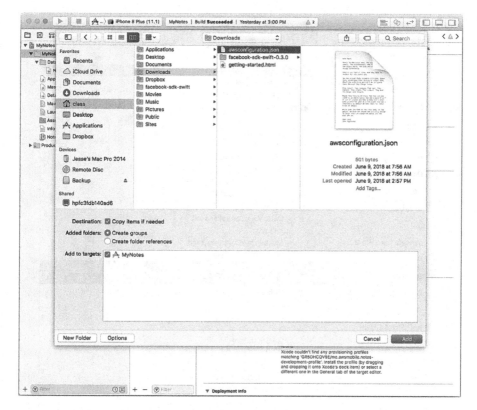

Figure 10-8. *Add the downloaded back end to your project*

Your project should now look like Figure 10-9, with the awsconfiguration.json file added. (It is easier to use the Xcode Add File command than the Finder to make sure your project files are in the right place.)

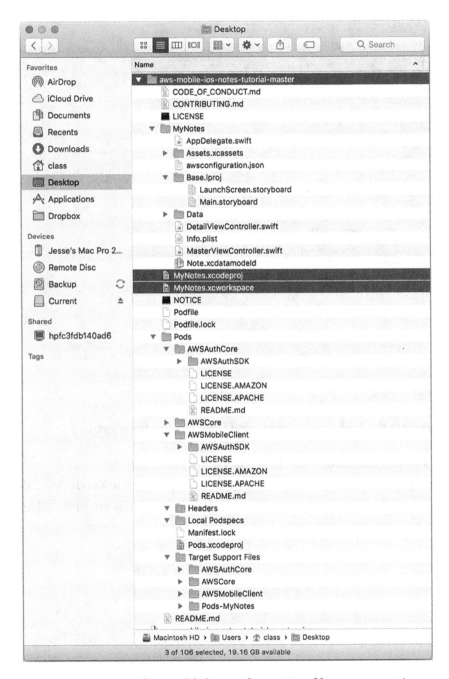

Figure 10-9. *Use Xcode to add the configuration file to your project*

Add the Pods

You now need to install CocoaPods if you haven't already done so for this or another project. To do so, use Terminal and input the following command:

```
sudo gem install cocoapods
```

You don't need to use a specific directory for this command.

Change the directory for Terminal to your app's folder. The simplest way to do this is to launch Terminal, type cd, and drag the aws-mobile-ios-notes-tutorial-master folder to complete the cd (change directory) command.

With the directory changed, type the following command to Terminal:

```
pod init
```

Your podfile will be created with the appropriate pods. Whenever you modify your podfile, install it with the following Terminal command:

```
pod install -- repo-update
```

This will move the project into an Xcode workspace as described in Chapter 3.

While you are in Xcode, check the General settings for your app, as shown in Figure 10-10. You will probably see errors related to the signing and provisioning profile settings. Change the bundle identifier and team to your own settings.

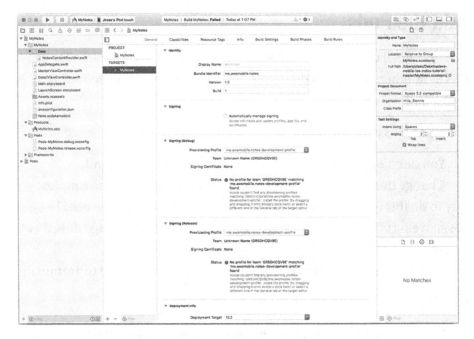

Figure 10-10. *Change the settings for your app*

You should be able to build and run your app now. As you can see in Figure 10-11, the pods will download necessary components. The download and build may take a few minutes, so be patient.

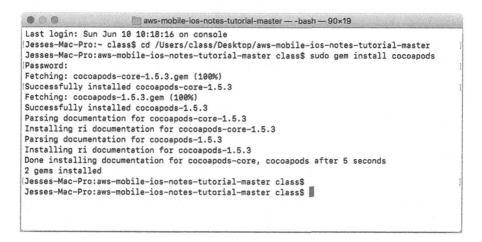

Figure 10-11. *Install CocoaPods for AWS*

Note   While the app is building, you may notice some error messages. Wait until the build is finished because they may disappear as further components are downloaded.

Summary

This chapter has showed you how to begin putting your AWS/iOS app together. In the next chapter, you'll start to actually use the integrated app.

PART V

Using RxSwift

CHAPTER 11

Getting Into Code

There are two types of developers in the world: those who want to get into the code first and then learn how it's working, and those who want to learn how things will work before they get into the code. Just to make things interesting, an individual developer may work in one mode or the other, switching back and forth for a sense of variety or depending on what issues need attention.

If you feel like starting with the background information, start with Chapter 12, "Thinking Reactively," and then come back to this chapter. Alternatively, keep reading this chapter to get yourself started with some very basic RxSwift code and then follow on with Chapter 12.

In this chapter, you'll find the basics of working with RxSwift:

- **Getting Started** will show you what you need on the hardware and software side of things.

- **Installing RxSwift from GitHub** will walk you through the download and installation process.

- **Using the RxSwift Playground** will show you how to write your first RxSwift code in Swift Playgrounds.

© Jesse Feiler 2018
J. Feiler, *Beginning Reactive Programming with Swift*,
https://doi.org/10.1007/978-1-4842-3621-5_11

Tip   If you haven't used Swift Playgrounds before, you'll find enough of the basics to use it in this book. However, you'll find out much more in *Learn Computer Science with Swift: Computation Concepts, Programming Paradigms, Data Management, and Modern Component Architectures with Swift and Playgrounds* and in *Exploring Swift Playgrounds: The Fastest and Most Effective Way to Learn to Code and to Teach Others to Use Your Code.* Both are by Jesse Feiler and are published by Apress.

Getting Started

The minimal getting-started things to know are:

- RxSwift itself is an open source implementation of the reactive programming library for Swift. You can download it freely from GitHub (the steps to do so are described in this chapter).

- Reactive programming lets you handle asynchronous processing easily.

- To implement the paradigm, reactive programming uses basic terms:

  - *Observables* are items that can be observed. When they change, those changes are visible to components that *subscribe* to the observable in question.

  - *Observers* observe observables.

These terms and concepts will be explored further in Chapter 12 and subsequent chapters of this book.

One other point to know from the start is that the reactive programming paradigm is often referred to as *Rx*.

With those basics, you now know enough to get started with RxSwift. You will need the following:

- A Mac running Xcode 9 or later. Xcode 9 is the integrated development environment (IDE) for developing apps on iOS and macOS. It also is the tool that Apple engineers use to build iOS and macOS themselves. Xcode is a free download from the Mac App Store. Check the system requirements for Xcode: those are the requirements you'll need to work with RxSwift.

- An Internet connection so that you can log on to GitHub. If you don't have one, you can do the download from GitHub onto a portable computer or drive and then copy the downloaded files onto your Mac.

Installing RxSwift from GitHub

GitHub is the default repository for most code today, including many collaborative and open source projects. You can register for a GitHub account that is private (many companies and individuals do this), but a private GitHub account has most of the same features as a public one.

Tip   Projects on GitHub are in source code *repositories* (often referred to as *repos*).

With Xcode 9, GitHub and source control in general are integrated more tightly with Xcode than ever before. As a result, if you have download instructions for RxSwift that pre-date Xcode 9, you may be directed to use a more complicated process than is necessary. This book uses the Xcode 9 integration and shows you a very simple way of integrating RxSwift with your Xcode projects.

Log on to `github.com` and search for `RxSwift` using the search field at the top of the window, shown in Figure 11-1. Remember that GitHub is a dynamically updated archive, so the files you download may differ over time. Periodically, the entire GitHub site is updated, but the functionality remains the same.

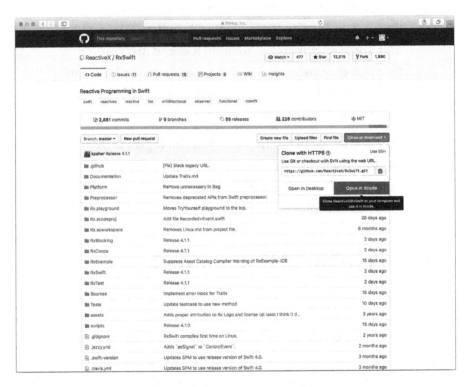

Figure 11-1. *Download RxSwift from GitHub*

If you have Xcode installed, the Clone or download button at the right will give you the options to download and open it either on your desktop or as a ZIP file. New in Xcode 9 is the option to open it in Xcode (but to use this option, you must enter your GitHub account credentials in Xcode ➤ Preferences ➤ Accounts). Choose the Xcode option. (If you don't see it, make sure that Xcode is installed and running and that you have entered your credentials in Xcode preferences.)

When you choose to open the code repository in Xcode, you'll be asked for permission, as you can see in Figure 11-2.

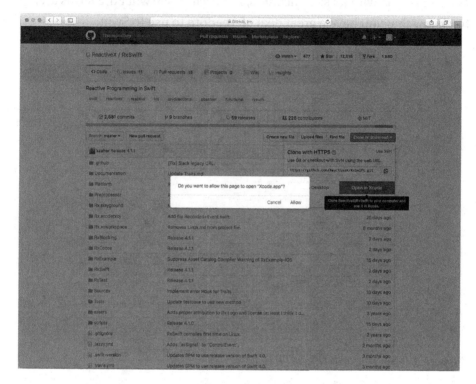

Figure 11-2. *Agree to let Xcode open the repository*

The RxSwift playground is part of the download. You start with it because the first time you run it, your downloaded files will be built as you follow the instructions in the following section of this book. Among the files that you have downloaded will be `Rx.xcworkspace`. A workspace can contain multiple Xcode projects, which is the case with this one. Make sure you open `Rx.xcworkspace` (the workspace) and not the project contained within it (`Rx.xcodeproj`).

RxSwift is covered by the MIT license. The MIT icon just above the download buttons shows you that license in detail, as you can see in Figure 11-3. As with all such licenses, review it to see what the terms are, but know that you have a great deal of freedom to use RxSwift.

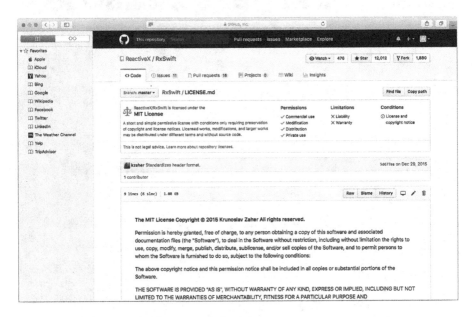

Figure 11-3. *Review the MIT license*

Using the RxSwift Playground

With the download completed, show the project navigator, as you can see in Figure 11-4. You may have to open the Rx folder and the Rx.playground folder within it. Select Table_of_Contents, as shown in Figure 11-4.

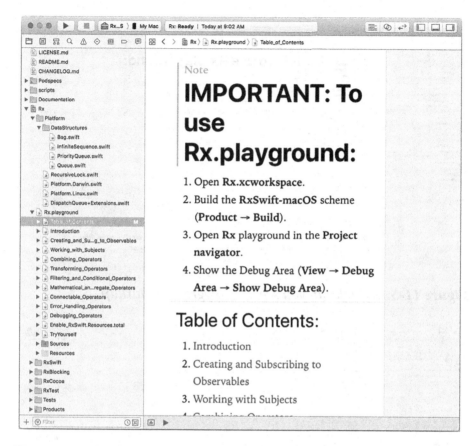

Figure 11-4. *Use Rx.Playground*

Select RxSwift-macOS from the Rx.playground folder and build it as described in Figure 11-4. You're ready to go on. (Note that step 2 lets you build the playground using the RxSwift-macOS scheme. There is more information on this in the following pages.)

Looking at a Formatted Playground

Playgrounds support markup code, and now is a good time to quickly explore that. By default, you will see the markup in the file (as shown in Figures 11-5 and 11-6).

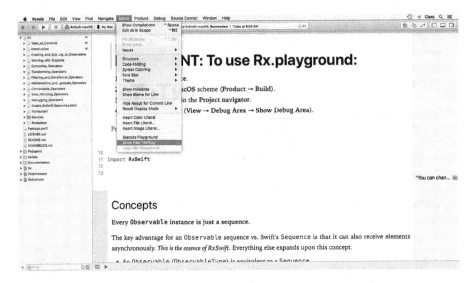

Figure 11-5. *By default, you see the playground markup*

Figure 11-6. *Switch between raw code and markup*

If you want to look at the raw code, you can use Editor ➤ Show Raw Markup, as illustrated in Figure 11-5. After you do that, you'll see the raw code, which is shown in Figure 11-6. Compare the two images to see the difference.

Don't worry about this. When you're building your own playgrounds it's useful to use markup, but you don't have to do so. If you do want to explore markup for playgrounds, there is more information in the Markup Formatting Reference at `https://developer.apple.com/library/content/documentation/Xcode/Reference/xcode_markup_formatting_ref/index.html#//apple_ref/doc/uid/TP40016497`. Note that the document covers markup for Quick Help as well as for Swift Playgrounds, so some formatting is only available to one or the other.

Follow the instructions shown in Figure 11-4. Open the Rx project as shown in Figure 11-7.

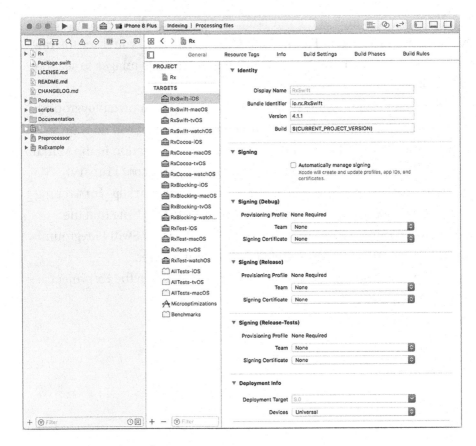

Figure 11-7. *Open the Rx targets*

Use the scheme menu at the top of the workspace window to select an RxSwift-mac OS destination, as you can see in Figure 11-8.

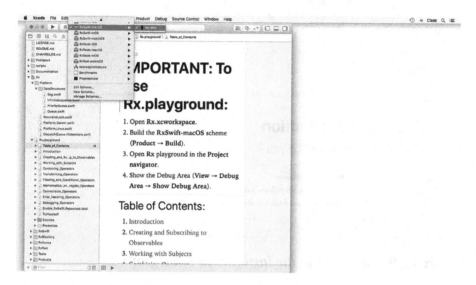

Figure 11-8. *Select the scheme*

The playground lets you experiment with live code. Don't worry for now about what the syntax does; just add a print statement, as shown in Figure 11-9. As you add new lines (even blank lines) to the playground, they will be numbered automatically.

Figure 11-9. *Add code to the Introduction playground*

Tip   You can add code to a playground whether or not markup is shown.

At the bottom of the playground window you can see the *debug area*, which displays output from the playground. (If you don't see it, choose View ► Debug Area ► Show Debug Area.) As you type, the playground will track your key strokes to identify errors. In Figure 11-10 you can see an error message that may appear as you are typing. Error messages like this will appear and disappear as you type and the playground analyzes your code (and possible errors).

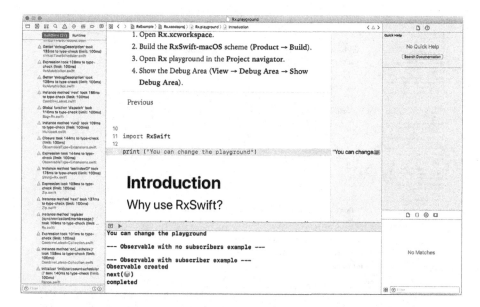

Figure 11-10. *The playground watches for errors*

You can experiment with additional code, as shown in Figure 11-11.

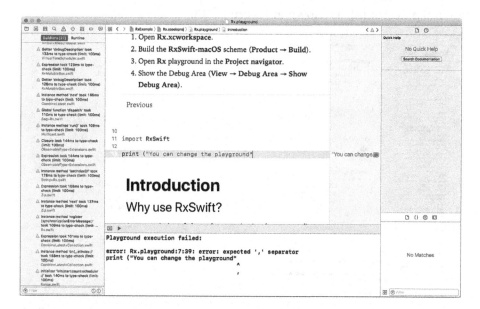

Figure 11-11. *The playground can catch errors quickly*

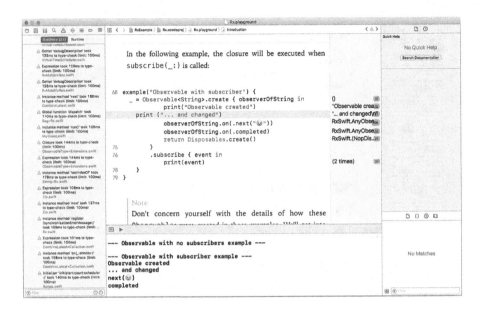

Figure 11-12. *Explore the playground with your own code*

If you remove any code you have added, you should be back to the original playground, as shown in Figure 11-13.

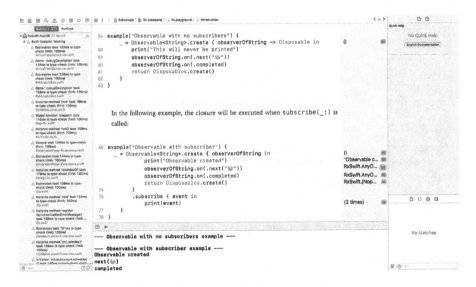

Figure 11-13. *Revert to the original playground*

Summary

You should now have RxSwift installed in Xcode. You can reference it from a playground or from regular Swift code in your app. When you want to add RxSwift to another playground or Xcode project, just follow the same steps you have seen here.

You'll see this in action later in the book, but first it's time to look at what's happening behind the scenes in RxSwift.

CHAPTER 12

Thinking Reactively

This chapter will help you put the concept of reactive programming in context with other programming styles, patterns, and paradigms. In the simplest non-jargon description, reactive programming is programming that makes it possible to easily handle modern software projects and apps that are likely to involve multiple users working at the same time with the same data.

Half a century ago it was possible to think of programming in the style of Hello World (the first program many people learned in classes). In Hello World, you type in a few lines of code (one to three, depending on formatting), and the program displays or prints the text, "Hello World."

More sophisticated programs in this vein allow users to interact with a Hello World program by typing in a word or phrase that the program will work with. Thus, the transcript of a sophisticated version of Hello World might look like this:

```
Good Morning. What is your name?
Jesse
Good Morning, Jesse
```

The sophistication of the program lies not only in the fact that the user can interact with it, but also in the fact that the program can determine whether to greet the user with Good Morning or Good Afternoon.

© Jesse Feiler 2018
J. Feiler, *Beginning Reactive Programming with Swift*,
https://doi.org/10.1007/978-1-4842-3621-5_12

Today, we are looking at much more complex systems that involve multiple users who have expectations of real-time updates so that they can see and participate in the activities of friends and colleagues. The tools we used in the days when we thought that Good Morning (instead of Good Afternoon) was great are stressed when we need to deal with these more complex systems.

This chapter will give you an overview of the tools that we need to use today (particularly those involved in RxSwift) as well as the terminology that is used to describe the tools and the products we are creating.

What Are We Developing?

In the earliest days of computers, the instructions to the computers were called *programs*. Groups of programs were often combined into *systems* in which the individual programs sometimes interacted and, in other cases, where they addressed issues related to the data involved in the programs.

The earliest programs were run by computer operators and schedulers. During the 1970s, when time-sharing and networks became available, a single large mainframe computer could be used for multiple programs running more or less simultaneously. In this environment, the running of programs devolved to users who started to use *application programs* that were designed to be run without technical assistance from schedulers and programmers. (Examples of early application programs were spreadsheets like VisiCalc and the first word-processing programs.)

Application programs designed for use by users rather than by computer specialists were gradually referred to as *applications* to distinguish them from the programs that run the computers themselves, which were often called *system programs*.

With the advent of smartphones, application programs got a further name simplification: *apps*. For a brief period of time, some people attempted to distinguish between application programs (for personal computers) and apps (for mobile devices), but that distinction never caught on (fortunately!).

Tip   There's more information on the earliest programs in *History of Programming Languages*, edited by Richard L. Wexelblat, published by Academic Press (ISBN 978-0127450407), which covers languages up to 1980 (that is, before C). A second volume, *History of Programming Languages II*, edited by Thomas J. Bergin and Richard G. Gibson, is published by Addison-Wesley Professional (ISBN 978-0201895025). It covers languages post-1980—languages including C, Smalltalk, ALGOL, and C++.

Today, we are seeing the functionality of apps being packaged in new ways, such as extensions in Cocoa and Cocoa Touch. The technologies and user interfaces are evolving rapidly, but in this book, the end product of development is generally referred to as an app or program even though it may be an extension.

The process of creating an app or program is referred to as *coding* (the original term from the early days of computers that has come back into fashion) or *programming*. *Developing* is the term often used to describe the production of an app or program together with its documentation, promotional or marketing materials, and training and sustainability tools.

Approaches to Programming

There are several overlapping ways of describing and categorizing development today. This section will provide you with a quick overview of some of the key concepts and terminology that are relevant to RxSwift. There are many books and other resources available that you can use for further investigation. What is important now is for you to know what the concepts are that you need to use and understand.

Tip   Wikipedia is a great resource for more information on these topics because its community of updaters has a lot of members of the technology world who make it their business to keep the articles current.

The reasons for such a variety of frequently overlapping terminologies and concepts are beyond the scope of this book. Suffice it to say that a combination of fast-moving development projects along with the need to provide detailed technical descriptions and marketing promotions of tools as well as end products have helped to provide what sometimes seems like an endless smorgasbord of jargon.

The terms and concepts can be divided into three groups, each of which is described more fully later in this chapter:

- **Programming paradigms** describe programming languages. When a user runs a program or app, it is unlikely that he or she will know what programming language it is written with, much less which paradigm(s) in that language are used. A specific language may use several programming paradigms.

- **Design patterns** are ways in which recurring tasks needed in object-oriented programming can be implemented. They may be visible to the user in the performance of the app, but they also may be strictly internal. Because they are designed to be used in object-oriented programming, they can be implemented in any language that supports the object-oriented paradigm. A given app or program may use multiple design patterns (or none at all).

- **Processing configurations** are the ways in which computers and their major components, such as processors and memory, are organized and connected. Although processing configurations are determined by the hardware on which an app runs, operating systems often provide features that minimize the differences so that a single configuration may at different times behave in different ways. (Look at the Grand Central Dispatch documentation in Cocoa and Cocoa Touch for an example of how this can work.)

Programming Paradigms

The main programming paradigms that matter to you if you are going to use RxSwift (and many other modern tools) are three that describe the program's structure and another three that describe how a program or app operates. (These are just the most common programming paradigms that are important for you in the RxSwift context.)

Structural Paradigms

The issue of programming paradigms began to be discussed in the late 1950s and 1960s when most of today's most commonly used languages were developed. It was necessary to describe them, and so these paradigms were identified and named. The main structural paradigms were reactions to the spaghetti-code programs that were frequently written. These programs consisted of line after line of code in one continuous program. Control could be transferred from one line to another because most lines were identified with a name or number. The term *spaghetti-code* was used to refer to the jumble of lines of code that were executed in complex and often unpredictable sequences.

To get rid of the spaghetti-code issues, these three concepts evolved:

- **Structured programming** uses subprograms (logical collections of statements) to provide a structure for the program. Depending on the language, these subprograms are called methods, functions, or procedures. When control is transferred, it is transferred from one subprogram to another rather than to a specific line of code.

- **Procedural** programming uses subprograms. They often take input data in the form of *parameters* and may return result values. At run time, the parameters of a subprogram are replaced by actual values—*arguments*.

- **Object-oriented (OOP)** programming lets you describe objects that can encapsulate both data and functionality (or both or neither). Objects can contain subprograms such as functions or methods. Often, objects correspond to real-world concepts such as a customer, a place, or an idea.

Operational Paradigms

These paradigms describe how the commands are written.

- **Imperative** programs consist of instructions to the computer to carry out specific tasks in a specific order. *Conditional statements* such as *if* let you modify that order, but the essence of imperative programs is the imperative instructions. (This term is used in the same way that it is used in language.) Tools such as Reactive Extensions (ReactiveX) help imperative languages work with sequences of data that may be either synchronous or asynchronous, thus somewhat bridging the distinctions between the two techniques.

- **Declarative** programs declare what the results of operations should be. Whereas imperative programs specify what is done as well as how it should be done, declarative program paradigms specify only what is done: the program or operating system is tasked with doing it in the most appropriate manner. Declarative programming languages include instructions designed to make it clear what these end results should be.

- **Functional** programs are a subset of declarative programs. They require that the program components be the sole determinants of the results of an operation such as a procedure or function. In other words, global variables and environmental settings are not used within the functions of a functional programming paradigm.

You can find a comparison of common programming paradigms on Wikipedia: `https://en.wikipedia.org/wiki/Comparison_of_programming_paradigms`.

Design Patterns

Design patterns are patterns or routines that can be used in similar situations. You can find them in many places, including a pattern in a house for how doors and locks are configured as well as in software. When used in the context that includes RxSwift, the term refers to a book that was published in 1994 and refers to design patterns in object-oriented software.

Tip   *Design Patterns: Elements of Reusable Object-Oriented Software* by Erich Gamma, Richard Helm, Ralph Johnson, and John Vlissides with a foreword by Grady Booch is published by Addison-Wesley Professional (ISBN-13 978-0201633610). The authors are often referred to as *the gang of four.*

The design patterns are divided into three categories:

- **Creational** design patterns are used to create objects.

- **Structural** design patterns are used for purposes such as connecting two objects.

- **Behavioral** design patterns are used to manage behavior and processing. ReactiveX uses the iterator and observer design patterns:

  - **Iterator**. This pattern lets you traverse some structure to get the next element (the pattern lets you specify what the sequence is).

  - **Observer**. With this pattern, you define a one-to-many relationship between an observer (one) and observed elements (many or none). It is a key feature that the observed element(s) doesn't know anything about the observer. An observed element *publishes* a change, and any observers receive a notification, but the observed element doesn't need to directly notify any observers.

Processing Configurations

The third collection of terms and concepts, processing configurations, is one that many developers skip over. What happens inside the processors is something that we take for granted. Simple apps such as Hello World are no longer good models for the code that we need to write, and the idea of a computer as a single device is also outdated. Almost every smartphone today runs with multiple cores—that is, multiple processors. Operating systems designed to run on such multi-core devices can perform several tasks at the same time.

What follows is a very high-level conceptual overview of multiprocessing. The operating systems allow a task to run on whatever core is available, and it can run as if there's only one core. To work around slow devices (printers, networks, and so forth), a task can be quickly stopped and packaged with its code and resources; that stopped task can then be put aside while something else executes.

The ability to pick up a task and move it aside is generalized beyond just waiting for a slow device. If a task can run independently of other tasks, it can run on one core while some other task runs on the first core.

With such use of multiple cores, the operating system and, to a lesser extent, the task software must be able to be split into independent tasks that can be run on separate cores. To get the most out of the available cores, it is important to keep track of what memory is required for each task as well as to provide a mechanism for synchronizing the tasks at points where they can (or cannot) share memory.

In thinking about this in terms of ReactiveX, it's necessary to distinguish between tasks or parts of tasks that can run independently (*asynchronously*) and those that must run in coordination (*synchronously*).

The goal of system software designers is to make multiprocessing possible with as little intervention by the app developer as possible. It should just happen . . . in an ideal world. With the introduction of Grand Central Dispatch (GCD) in OS X 10.6 (2009) and iOS 4 (2010), existing concurrency code in the operating systems was rewritten to make the use of multi-core devices possible with little difficulty to developers. What is key to the successful use of GCD is the use of queues of tasks. You add tasks to queues, and GCD takes over.

It is important to remember that the efficient use of multiple cores relies on developers' using queues properly. Fortunately, ReactiveX incorporates most of the core manipulation into its RxSwift objects.

For now, just remember that asynchronous processing is built into RxSwift.

Introducing Reactive Programming

There's a commonly repeated description of reactive programming on Wikipedia: "reactive programming is an asynchronous programming paradigm concerned with data streams and the propagation of change." That is true, but it requires a substantial understanding of the background terms, such as *asynchronous programming paradigm*, *data stream*, and *propagation of change*. You have an overview of asynchronous programming in the previous section. For now, consider a data stream to be just that—a flow of data that can be on its way to a printer, communication device, or other part of the app. *Propagation of change* refers to the ability of an app to respond to a change in its environment and pass that change on appropriately. (That's exactly the meaning in English of the words—it's not specifically a technical concept.)

Focusing on ReactiveX

The basic description of ReactiveX is concise in its documentation: "The Observer pattern done right." That, too, requires some background knowledge, but the focus is just on one thing rather than the three in the previous description: the observer pattern. The fuller description is

"ReactiveX is a combination of the best ideas from the Observer pattern, the Iterator pattern, and functional programming." The website is at http://reactivex.io. A further clarification is, "ReactiveX is more than an API; it's an idea and a breakthrough in programming."

Note   Observer and iterator patterns as well as functional programming are discussed in the previous section.

The heart of RxSwift (and many other reactive programming projects such as RxJava, RxJS, Rx.Net, RxScala, and RxClojure) is the ReactiveX library. ReactiveX itself is a collection of open source projects. The ReactiveX project is also open source, licensed under the Creative Commons Attribution license. Code samples are licensed under the BSD license.

Summary

This chapter has provided an overview of the technologies on which RxSwift relies. Nothing is new here or specific to RxSwift. In the chapters that follow, you will see code that implements these design patterns in RxSwift, and you will find real-life examples of their use.

At this point, you've seen how to download RxSwift from GitHub and how to build it in Xcode. It's time to look at the basics of the code you will use.

CHAPTER 13

Exploring the Basic RxCode

Having explored the basics of RxSwift in a playground (Chapter 11) and learned the underpinnings of the technology (Chapter 12), it's time to look at RxSwift at work in an app. This chapter will show you how to take code that you can download from GitHub and turn it into an app.

RxSwift implements reactive programming, and that's what the app in this chapter will demonstrate. It starts very basically: The app reacts to events that the user generates. That type of app can be created easily using notifications within the app because the app generates both the event/ stimulus and the reaction/response.

This very simple structure is useful for exploring the structure and syntax of RxSwift. Once you have the basics implemented, you can move onto the kind of reaction that most people think of when they think of reactive programming—reaction to external events from outside the app.

This chapter will show you how to put one of the sample apps built in Xcode into the downloaded RxSwift Xcode files. Having done that, you'll have the two components you need: RxSwift and Xcode working together.

Note   You need Xcode installed to continue.

© Jesse Feiler 2018
J. Feiler, *Beginning Reactive Programming with Swift*,
https://doi.org/10.1007/978-1-4842-3621-5_13

Overview of ReactiveX/RxSwift–Xcode Integration

There are several ways to integrate Xcode and ReactiveX/RxSwift. Which method you use depends on your experience and preferences. The type of app that you're building is less important than your preferences. The starting point is the GitHub repository for ReactiveX/RxSwift. Chapter 11 showed you how to download it and use the Swift playground that's part of it. You need part of that repo to integrate with your own app. One of the benefits of using GitHub is that it changes as people use and modify the archives. As a result, the GitHub version you see may differ from the version described in this chapter.

There are a number of techniques available in the GitHub repo for integration with your own app. As of this writing (in 2018), the integration methods are the following:

- CocoaPods is available at `http://cocoapods.org/`. It is designed for managing the distribution and dependencies of source code for Xcode projects.

- Carthage, available at `https://github.com/Carthage/Carthage/releases`, is more closely integrated with Xcode and Swift than CocoaPods, and many people find it somewhat simpler to use.

- Swift Package Manager (SPM) is part of the Swift project and is available at `https://swift.org/package-manager/`. Its integration with Swift is more thorough than that of CocoaPods or Carthage, but it is not yet as widely used as CocoaPods.

In this chapter, the process of integrating the files from GitHub will be described based simply on the archive files and without the use of CocoaPods, Carthage, or SPM. This can be a simpler path for beginners.

Start from the RxSwift Download

Begin by downloading the current version of RxSwift from GitHub, as described in Chapter 1. The critical step is the download from GitHub into Xcode. Figure 13-1 reminds you of this step. It is easiest to download it into a new folder. Later on, you can rearrange files, but to make certain that what you have downloaded will build and run on your Mac and your version of Xcode, keep the installation simple.

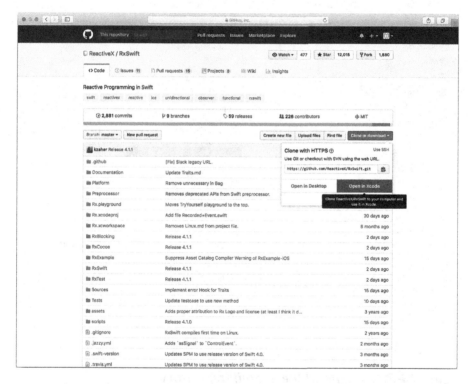

Figure 13-1. *Download the GitHub RxSwift code directly into Xcode*

The files you have downloaded will look somewhat like the files you see in Figure 13-2. Remember that this archive is growing and changing all the time, but the basic structure is constant. Make certain that you have Rs.xcodeproj and Rx.xcworkspace. If you don't, you have the wrong archive.

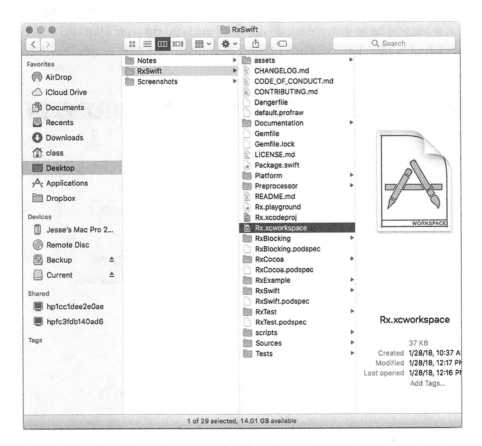

Figure 13-2. Download the RxSwift repository

Explore the Workspace and Playground

Now, open the workspace (Rx.xcworkspace) with Xcode, as shown
in Figure 13-3. You may have to do some rearranging and opening or
closing of groups. What you normally see is shown in Figure 13-3: It's the
Rx.playground. Look particularly at the project navigator at the left side
of the window.

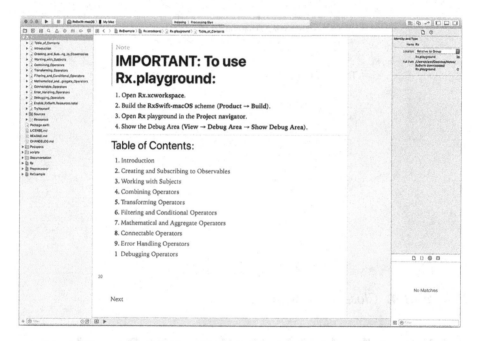

Figure 13-3. *Open the Rx.workspace and then Rx.playground*

Close the playground groups so that the first item you see in `Package.swift` as you see in Figure 13-4.

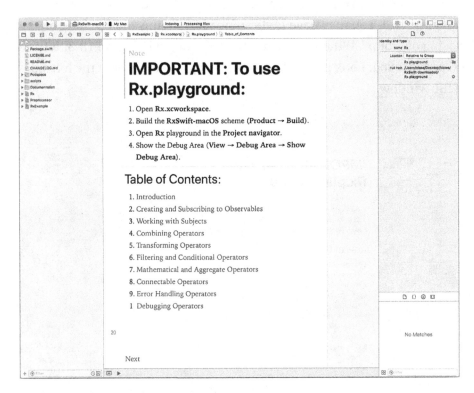

Figure 13-4.   *Close the playground*

Adding a Project to the RxSwift Download

Now, add a project to the workspace. To keep things organized, it's easiest at this point to click in the blank area at the bottom of the project navigator so that your new project will go there. (You can rearrange it later.)

Create the project by choosing New ➤ Project to select your template, as shown in Figure 13-5. For this basic example, the Single View App in the iOS tab is perfect.

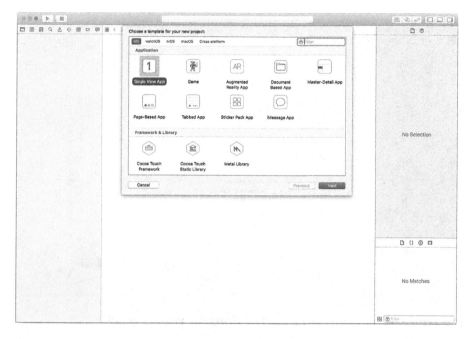

Figure 13-5. *Choose a new project template*

As is always the case, when you click Next you need to name your project and locate it on disk. For simplicity, place it in the same folder that you used to download the RxSwift repository. Name it `Basic` to match the screenshots in this book. The project navigator should now look like it does in Figure 13-6.

Do not use Core Data, Unit Tests, or UI Tests when you create the project (there are checkboxes for them at the bottom of the options sheet, as shown in Figure 13-6).

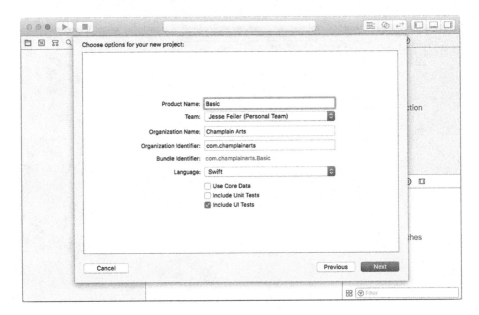

Figure 13-6. *Set the name and options for your project*

When prompted for a location to store the new project, place it in the Rx workspace and in whatever group you want, as you can see in Figure 13-7.

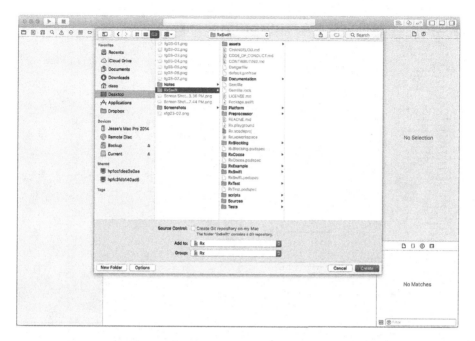

Figure 13-7. *Place the new project into the Rx workspace and whatever group you want*

Drag the new project (`Basic`, in this example) to the top—or bottom—of the project navigator so it's easy to spot.

Tip If you want to create a new empty group folder for it before you add it, you'll save yourself a step, but for many people that seems to be out of sequence.

Figure 13-8 shows the project now.

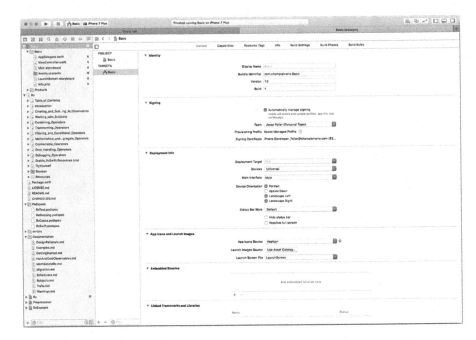

Figure 13-8. *Your new project is now part of the workspace*

If you look at the files on disk, you'll see that your project is in the right place, as you can see in Figure 13-9.

Figure 13-9. *Check that your new project files are in the right place*

Note   Make certain that the files are in the right place. If they're not
in the folder for your project, things will work perfectly well as long
as you don't move the project. When you move the project elsewhere
(such as to a MacBook) the project may break. You can move the new
project files separately as long as you remember to do so, but it's
easier to keep the whole project together.

Building Your RxSwift-enhanced Project

Before moving on, make certain that your project builds and runs. (This is always a good idea when creating a project from a template.) As you can see in Figure 13-8, at the top of the window, you can build and run the project for any installed simulator or for a device. When you run it on a simulator, you should see the result shown in Figure 13-10. (Yes, Figure 13-10 is what you should see: no error messages and nothing else. In the next section, you'll see how to add a label to confirm that your app is truly running.)

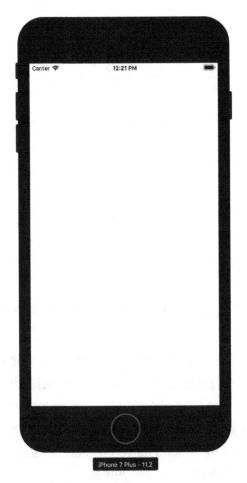

Figure 13-10. *Your project should run now*

Modify the Project

The purpose of this section is to make certain that you can modify, build, and run the RxSwift-enhanced project you have created. Locate main. storyboard in the project (it's at the top of Figure 13-8). Add a label to the window just as you would do with any project in Interface Builder. The storyboard with the label is shown in Figure 13-11.

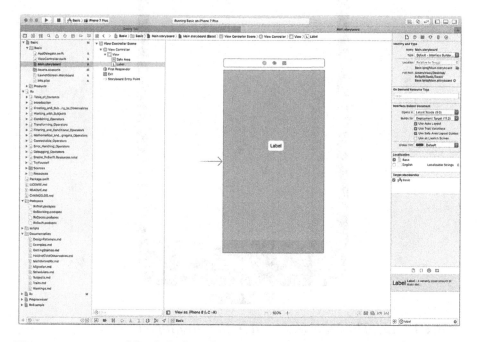

Figure 13-11. *Add a label to the storyboard*

Run the project again, and you should see your label in the interface, as shown in Figure 13-12.

Figure 13-12. *The label is shown in the running project*

Summary

At this point, you should be able to download RxSwift from GitHub and add your own project to it. As with most projects you will create, you will probably start from one of the built-in Xcode templates, and that is what has been done.

Now, it's time to move on to a more complex project—one that you can use as a starting point for many of your own RxSwift projects.

CHAPTER 14

Build a ReactiveX/RxSwift App

In the last three chapters, you have seen the basics of RxSwift and reactive programming as well as how to create a very basic app using the ReactiveX/RxSwift repository from GitHub. This chapter will move further so that you can build a small app that uses basic reactive features.

You will build a simple app that lets you choose an item from a list, as you can see in Figure 14-1. This is a typical beginning ReactiveX app that you will find in many variations across the Internet. What you are looking at is a UISearchBar and a UITableView. The table view is seeded with six items in the app. You can type into the search bar to select one or more of the items. The app is watching you; if you type F, you'll see the three forts. If you type O, you'll see Oval, and if you type G, you won't see anything, because none of the names starts with G. The app will be called DemoList.

You can implement this without RxSwift by adding a delegate to the search bar so that you can keep track of what is being typed, but using RxSwift can be a more straightforward way of implementing the process. Furthermore, if you decide to move on to a more complex app in which the table view is automatically populated with choices that depend on external conditions, you'll be ready to implement those features.

© Jesse Feiler 2018
J. Feiler, *Beginning Reactive Programming with Swift*,
https://doi.org/10.1007/978-1-4842-3621-5_14

Note   The items in the list represent places in Plattsburgh, New York.

An important point to note is that Figure 14-1 shows DemoList running on an actual device (an iPod Touch, as you can see from the status bar).

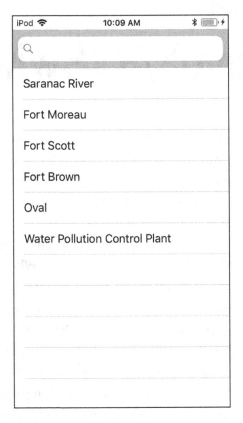

Figure 14-1. *Build DemoList*

When you run an app on the iOS simulator, the status bar will show a generic carrier, as you can see in Figure 14-2.

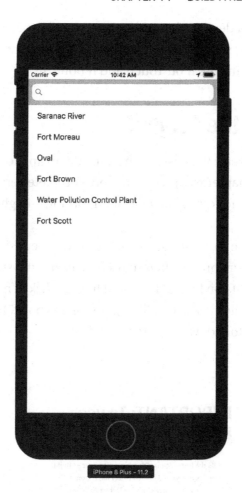

Figure 14-2. *Running on the iOS simulator*

The simulator is updated to be able to support many versions of iOS, but there remain certain features of iOS that are not identical when running on a device or the simulator. For example, on the simulator, iCloud synchronization is triggered by a menu command (Debug ➤ Trigger iCloud Sync), and various other aspects of the operating system function differently on the simulator than they do on actual devices. That is true of features and also of projects that are built from multiple files. When they are built in one environment such as Xcode, files and frameworks that are necessary may be available, but then are not available when they app is

185

moved to an actual device. The safest way to avoid deployment surprises is to use a device for testing frequently during development. (Popular devices for this kind of testing are iPod Touch and iPhone SE.)

Setting Up the Project

In Chapter 13, you saw the basics of how to add an app to the downloaded repository. This chapter will present a more complete version that you can use repeatedly for other apps. Most important, it begins to use RxSwift features and syntax.

If you follow the steps to download the GitHub repository, you'll have the most current version. The files may change, and the structure may change as well, so if you look at the list of files on disk, it may be slightly different than the files you see in the figures of this book. Figure 14-3 shows the GitHub repository downloaded in Xcode.

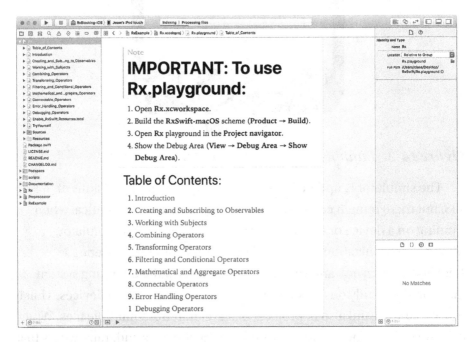

Figure 14-3. Downloaded ReactiveXRxSwift repository in Xcode

You may have to open or close some of the disclosure triangles to see the files. What is most important to notice here is the playground files. They may be in an Rx project at the top of the list (or they may have moved). Figure 14-3 shows you the four steps to take:

1. Open Rx.xcworkspace

2. Build the RxSwift-macOS scheme (Product ➤ Build).

3. Open Rx playground in the Project navigator

4. Show the Debug area (View ➤ Debug Area ➤ Show Debug Area).

If you can't build it as described in the four steps, there is probably something wrong with your download.

Note   The build process for the playground can take several minutes to complete. Watch the status bar at the top of the window to see the status of indexing, which is what will often take a while. The indexing status message is shown in Figure 14-3.

Once you have built the playground, you can delete the files, but it's a good idea to keep the full downloaded archive in a safe place. After you have deleted the playground files, your project may look like Figure 14-4, in which all of the playground files are removed. This may be a version of RxSwift that you use as a starting place for various projects that don't need the playground files.

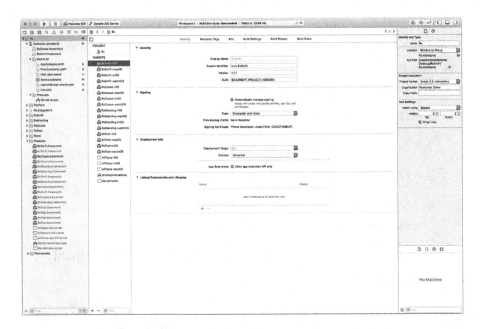

Figure 14-4. *GitHub repo without playground project*

The Rx project toward the bottom of the repo is the main project, rather than the playground that you have deleted at this point. If you select the Rx project and look at the targets, as shown in Figure 14-4, you'll see the components of ReactiveX.

For basic work with ReactiveX, you need to compile RxCocoa and RxSwift for the device on which you want to run the project. You can do that from the schema at the top left of the window, shown in Figure 14-4.

Tip   To save time, you can build RxSwift and RxCocoa for a generic iOS device, as shown in Figure 14-4. These are needed to support your app.

Once you have built RxCocoa and RxSwift, you can create your new app. This example (shown previously in Figure 14-1) can be called DemoList. Choose File ➤ New ➤ Project and then select Single View App, as shown in Figure 14-5.

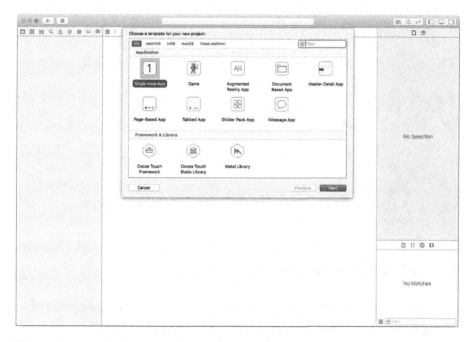

Figure 14-5. *Create a new Single View App project*

Set the project options and name, as shown in Figure 14-6.

Figure 14-6. *Name the new project and set its options*

When it comes time to save your new project, you have the option of adding it to your existing project, as you can see in Figure 14-7.

Figure 14-7. *Save your new project*

Choose the option to add it to your existing project or workspace, as shown in Figure 14-8.

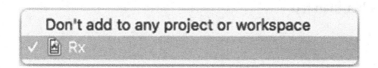

Figure 14-8. *Add your new project to the existing project or workspace*

As always when you create a new project, try to build and run it. Bearing in mind the issues of devices versus simulator, a good test at this point is to run it both on a device and in a simulator before you enter any code. (If you do run it, remember that the storyboard is blank, so seeing a blank screen is the expected behavior. You can add a label or image as described previously to verify your app.)

Add ReactiveX

So far, this is basically the process you've seen before for adding onto the downloaded repository. Now, it's time to add ReactiveX.

Build RxCocoa and RxSwift

You will need RxCocoa and RxSwift to be built before you start. If you haven't done so already, build them as shown in Figure 14-4. Remember that you can use a generic iOS device for these builds. After the builds, they will be listed in the Products group, as you can see in Figure 14-9. All of the available products will be listed. The ones that have been built will show in black rather than red.

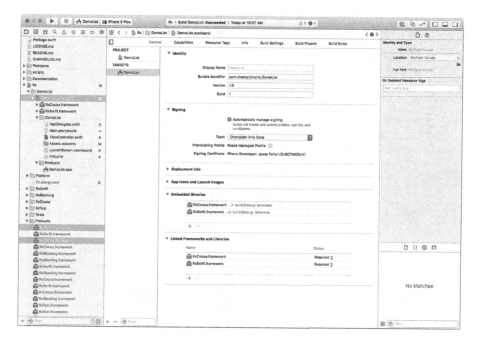

Figure 14-9. *Verify you have built RxSwift and RxCocoa*

Add RxSwift and RxCocoa to Your Project

Now, drag RxSwift and RxCocoa into the Embedded Binaries section on
the General tab of DemoList. If you drag them to Embedded Binaries, they
will also automatically be added to Linked Frameworks and Libraries.

Verify the Syntax

The acid test will be if you can reference the ReactiveX features in your
source code, and then if you can run your app and use them. They will be
needed in ViewController in the app template, so add `import` statements at
the top of the code, as shown in Figure 14-10.

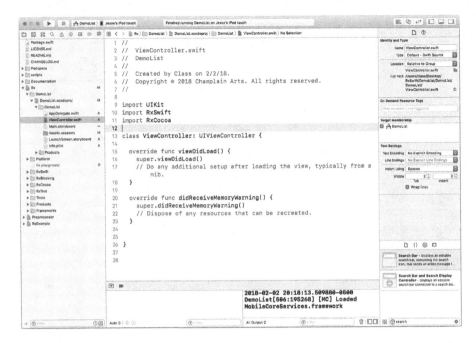

Figure 14-10. *Add import statements*

If something has gone wrong, you'll not be able to build your app. You may even get a syntax error as you type the import statements. If you do get errors, double-check the steps you have taken and keep an eye on the status bar at the top of the window to make certain that your indexing has completed. Be aware that as you are moving these files around and building the ReactiveX components, you may see errors that will go away as the project is fully indexed and built. Don't react to syntax errors too quickly.

Building the Storyboard

With your template-based project under way, you can start to build the storyboard. In short, you need to create a view controller with a search bar and a table (refer back to Figure 10-1 to see the result).

The steps for this process are the same basic Xcode and Interface Builder steps that you use in any project. Begin by opening the storyboard with your single view controller in it. Select the view controller and choose a translucent navigation bar for the top, as shown in Figure 14-11.

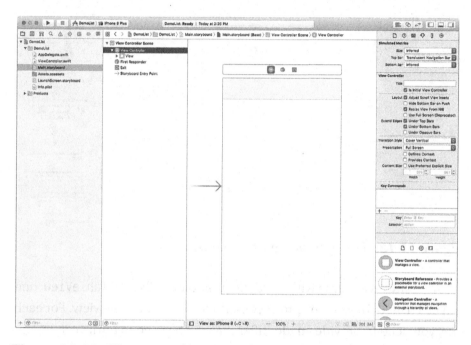

Figure 14-11. *Use a translucent navigation bar at the top of the view controller*

Add a UITableView to the view. With the table view selected, choose "Dynamic Prototypes" for the table view and specify one prototype, as you can see in Figure 14-12.

In ViewController, add references to the search bar and table view so that they are visible to your code at the top of ViewController:

```
@IBOutlet weak var searchBar: UISearchBar!
@IBOutlet weak var tableView: UITableView!
```

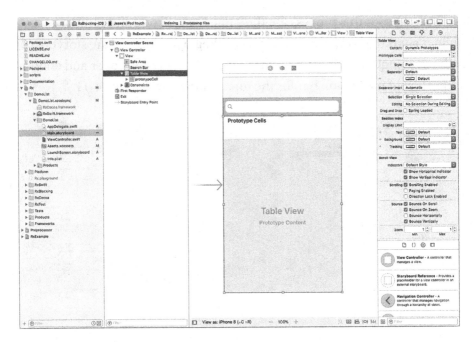

Figure 14-12. *Use dynamic prototype cells*

As is always the case with dynamic prototype cells in UITableView, one will be created for as many prototypes as you set in the table view. For each one, you need to provide an identifier that will be used to retrieve it. In Figure 14-12 you see prototypeCell used as the name of the prototype cell in the structure view at the left of the layout.

Adding the UITableView Code and Delegate

If you are following along, all you need to do now is to implement ViewController. No changes in the template are needed for AppDelegate, Assets.xcassets, Info.plist, or LaunchScreen.storyboard. The template itself makes some entries, but you don't change them.

You need to implement a DataSource for your table view. (A Delegate may need to be implemented later on.) The DataSource provides the data to the view controller. The two key methods for the data source are the same as you use in any UITableView.

Create two arrays in ViewController. items will be all possible items to be shown in the list, and itemsToShow will be the items from items that are shown. The declarations should look like this:

```
var itemsToShow = [String]()
let items = ["Saranac River", "Fort Moreau", "Oval", "Fort Brown",
  "Water Pollution Control Plant", "Fort Scott"]
```

(The strings in items are up to you.)

You also will need a declaration of a DisposeBag to manage your observer. This will automatically collect disposables generated in this object (ViewController), and when the object is deallocated and its deinit method is called, the disposables will be released.

```
let disposeBag = DisposeBag()
```

You will need to implement viewDidLoad as follows:

```
override func viewDidLoad() {
  super.viewDidLoad()
}
```

Two standard UITableView functions let you specify the number of items to be shown and what they are.

To specify the number of items to be shown, use numberOfRowsInSection. Return the count of itemsToShow so that the function looks like this:

```
func tableView (_ tableView: UITableView, numberOfRowsInSection
section: Int) -> Int {
  return itemsToShow.count
}
```

You format and return the cell to be displayed. You use the identifier for the prototype cell you want to use, and you set its textLabel to the relevant string from itemsToShow:

```
func tableView(_ tableView: UITableView, cellForRowAt
indexPath: IndexPath) ->
  UITableViewCell {

  let cell = tableView.dequeueReusableCell(withIdentifier:
  "prototypeCell",
    for: indexPath)
    cell.textLabel?.text = itemsToShow[indexPath.row]
    return cell
}
```

Finally, specify that ViewController conforms to the UITableViewDataSource protocol by changing the declaration as follows:

```
class ViewController: UIViewController, UITableViewDataSource {
```

In Interface Builder, connect the table view to the data source.

Implementing the ReactiveX Search Bar

The final section of code implements the search bar in viewDidLoad. What matters most are the following:

- An items array (it doesn't matter what the array types are as long as they are strings)

- An itemsToShow array (it starts as an empty String array)

- A tableView called tableView

This is one of features of functional programming: you don't need to worry about the specific data you're working with in many cases.

```
override func viewDidLoad() {
  super.viewDidLoad()
  // Do any additional setup after loading the view,
typically from a nib.
  searchBar
    .rx.text
    .orEmpty
    .subscribe(onNext: { [unowned self] query in
      self.itemsToShow = self.items.filter {
        $0.hasPrefix(query)
      }
      self.tableView.reloadData()
    })
}
```

Note   You may get a warning that `subscribe` is not used at this point: that is a warning, and you can continue for now.

Reviewing the Code

All told, your code is complete now. It should look like Listing 14-1.

Listing 14-1. Complete code for the view controller

```
import UIKit
import RxSwift
import RxCocoa
```

```swift
class ViewController: UIViewController, UITableViewDataSource {

  @IBOutlet weak var searchBar: UISearchBar!
  @IBOutlet weak var tableView: UITableView!

  var itemsToShow = [String]()
  let items = ["Saranac River", "Fort Moreau", "Oval", "Fort
  Brown",
    "Water Pollution Control Plant", "Fort Scott"]

  let disposeBag = DisposeBag()

  override func viewDidLoad() {
    super.viewDidLoad()
    // Do any additional setup after loading the view,
    typically from a nib.
    searchBar
      .rx.text
      .orEmpty
      .subscribe(onNext: { [unowned self] query in
        self.itemsToShow = self.items.filter {
          $0.hasPrefix(query)
        }
        self.tableView.reloadData()
      })
  }

  func tableView (_ tableView: UITableView,
numberOfRowsInSection section: Int) -> Int
  {
    return itemsToShow.count
  }
```

```
func tableView(_ tableView: UITableView, cellForRowAt
indexPath: IndexPath)
  -> UITableViewCell {
  let cell = tableView.dequeueReusableCell(withIdentifier:
  "prototypeCell",
    for: indexPath)
  cell.textLabel?.text = itemsToShow[indexPath.row]
  return cell
}

override func didReceiveMemoryWarning() {
  super.didReceiveMemoryWarning()
  // Dispose of any resources that can be recreated.
}
}
```

Summary

You should be able to run the app now. Open the project in Xcode and select DemoList to run.

Index

A, B

Acid test, 193
Amazon Web Services (AWS)
   account
      Mobile Hub, 126–127
      sign in, 125
   add pods, 135–136
   back end, 131–134
   with Cocoa
      cloud-based computing,
        102, 104
      and Cocoa Touch, 100–101
      data management, 108–109
      sharing data, 101–104
      users' expectations, 104–105
   create project, 130
   developer resources on, 107
   documentation for, 128–130
   login process
      accounts, 111–116
      creating organizations,
        116–117
      IAM tools, 117–120
      root user, 111–116
      Xcode, 121–122
   products, 108
   web-based technology, 105

Application programs, 158
App Store, 31
Asynchronous
      programming, 166
Authentication process, 4

C

Carthage, 170
Cloud computing, 127
Cocoa
   AWS (*see* Amazon Web
      Services (AWS))
   Core Data tool, 109
   SQLite, 109
CocoaPods
   GitHub repository, 17
   install, 18
   integration methods, 77, 170
   podfile, 17
   single-view app
      check directory, 22–23
      command line, 21
      create new folder, 19–20
      create new project, 19
      install command, 24
      podfile, 23–24
      review project, 20–21

© Jesse Feiler 2018
J. Feiler, *Beginning Reactive Programming with Swift*,
https://doi.org/10.1007/978-1-4842-3621-5

Printed in the United States
By Bookmasters